FOUR ARCHETYPES

from

The Collected Works of C. G. Jung

VOLUME 9, PART I

BOLLINGEN SERIES XX

FOUR
ARCHETYPES

MOTHER

REBIRTH

SPIRIT

TRICKSTER

C. G. JUNG

TRANSLATED BY R. F. C. HULL

BOLLINGEN SERIES

PRINCETON UNIVERSITY PRESS

First Princeton/Bollingen Paperback Edition, 1970

Third printing, 1973

Extracted from *The Archetypes and the Collective Unconscious,* Vol. 9, part I, of the *Collected Works of C. G. Jung.* All the volumes comprising the *Collected Works* constitute number XX in Bollingen Series, under the editorship of Herbert Read (d. 1968), Michael Fordham, and Gerhard Adler; executive editor, William McGuire.

LC Card 73-123079

ISBN 0-691-01766-2

Printed in the USA

EDITORIAL NOTE

The concept of archetypes and its correlate, that of the collective unconscious, are among the better known theories developed by Professor Jung. Their origins may be traced to his earliest publication, "On the Psychology and Pathology of So-called Occult Phenomena" (1902),* in which he described the fantasies of an hysterical medium. Intimations of the concepts can be found in many of his subsequent writings, and gradually tentative statements crystallized and were reformulated until a stable core of theory was established.

Volume 9 of the *Collected Works* consists of writings (from 1933 onward) describing and elaborating the two concepts. Part I, *The Archetypes and the Collective Unconscious,* is introduced by three essays establishing the theoretical basis, followed by others describing specific archetypes, including the four that compose this paperback selection.† The relation of the archetypes to the process of individuation and in particular to mandala symbolism is defined in essays in the last section. Part II of Volume 9, entitled *Aion* and published separately, is devoted to a long monograph on the symbolism of the self as revealed in the "Christian aeon."

For this paperback edition, a brief theoretical introduction is supplied by extracts from "Archetypes of the Collective Unconscious," the first essay in Volume 9, part I. The paragraph numbers of the *Collected Works* edition have been retained to facilitate reference, and a new index has been prepared. The bibliography includes only works relevant to this selection.

* In *Psychiatric Studies*, vol. 1 of the *Collected Works* (see list at end of this book).

† Two other essays, "The Psychology of the Child Archetype" and "The Psychological Aspects of the Kore," have been published in C.G. Jung and C. Kerényi, *Essays on a Science of Mythology* (Princeton/Bollingen Paperback no. 180).

v

TABLE OF CONTENTS

FOUR ARCHETYPES

INTRODUCTION[1]

1   The hypothesis of a collective unconscious belongs to the class of ideas that people at first find strange but soon come to possess and use as familiar conceptions. This has been the case with the concept of the unconscious in general. After the philosophical idea of the unconscious, in the form presented chiefly by Carus and von Hartmann, had gone down under the overwhelming wave of materialism and empiricism, leaving hardly a ripple behind it, it gradually reappeared in the scientific domain of medical psychology.

2   At first the concept of the unconscious was limited to denoting the state of repressed or forgotten contents. Even with Freud, who makes the unconscious—at least metaphorically—take the stage as the acting subject, it is really nothing but the gathering place of forgotten and repressed contents, and has a functional significance thanks only to these. For Freud, accordingly, the unconscious is of an exclusively personal nature,[2] although he was aware of its archaic and mythological thought-forms.

3   A more or less superficial layer of the unconscious is undoubtedly personal. I call it the *personal unconscious*. But this personal unconscious rests upon a deeper layer, which does not derive from personal experience and is not a personal acquisition but is inborn. This deeper layer I call the *collective unconscious*. I have chosen the term "collective" because this part of the unconscious is not individual but universal; in contrast to

1 [From "Archetypes of the Collective Unconscious," first published in the *Eranos-Jahrbuch 1934*, and later revised and published in *Von den Wurzeln des Bewusstseins* (Zurich, 1954), from which version the present translation is made. The translation of the original version, by Stanley Dell, in *The Integration of the Personality* (New York, 1939; London, 1940), has been freely consulted.—EDITORS.]
2 In his later works Freud differentiated the basic view mentioned here. He called the instinctual psyche the "id," and his "super-ego" denotes the collective consciousness, of which the individual is partly conscious and partly unconscious (because it is repressed).

the personal psyche, it has contents and modes of behaviour that are more or less the same everywhere and in all individuals. It is, in other words, identical in all men and thus constitutes a common psychic substrate of a suprapersonal nature which is present in every one of us.

4 Psychic existence can be recognized only by the presence of contents that are *capable of consciousness*. We can therefore speak of an unconscious only in so far as we are able to demonstrate its contents. The contents of the personal unconscious are chiefly the *feeling-toned complexes*, as they are called; they constitute the personal and private side of psychic life. The contents of the collective unconscious, on the other hand, are known as *archetypes*.

5 The term "archetype" occurs as early as Philo Judaeus,[3] with reference to the *Imago Dei* (God-image) in man. It can also be found in Irenaeus, who says: "The creator of the world did not fashion these things directly from himself but copied them from archetypes outside himself." [4] In the *Corpus Hermeticum*,[5] God is called τὸ ἀρχέτυπον φῶς (archetypal light). The term occurs several times in Dionysius the Areopagite, as for instance in *De caelesti hierarchia*, II, 4: "immaterial Archetypes," [6] and in *De divinis nominibus*, I, 6: "Archetypal stone." [7] The term "représentations collectives," used by Lévy-Bruhl to denote the symbolic figures in the primitive view of the world, could easily be applied to unconscious contents as well, since it means practically the same thing. Primitive tribal lore is concerned with archetypes that have been modified in a special way. They are no longer contents of the unconscious, but have already been changed into conscious formulae taught according to tradition, generally in the form of esoteric teaching. This last is a typical means of expression for the transmission of collective contents originally derived from the unconscious.

6 Another well-known expression of the archetypes is myth and fairytale. But here too we are dealing with forms that have received a specific stamp and have been handed down through

---

[3] *De opificio mundi*, I, 69. Cf. Colson/Whitaker trans., I, p. 55.

[4] *Adversus haereses* II, 7, 5: "Mundi fabricator non a semetipso fecit haec, sed de alienis archetypis transtulit." (Cf. Roberts/Rambaut trans., I, p. 139.)

[5] Scott, *Hermetica*, I, p. 140.　　[6] In Migne, *P.G.*, vol. 3, col. 144.

[7] Ibid., col. 595. Cf. *The Divine Names* (trans. by Rolt), pp. 62, 72.

long periods of time. The term "archetype" thus applies only indirectly to the "représentations collectives," since it designates only those psychic contents which have not yet been submitted to conscious elaboration and are therefore an immediate datum of psychic experience. In this sense there is a considerable difference between the archetype and the historical formula that has evolved. Especially on the higher levels of esoteric teaching the archetypes appear in a form that reveals quite unmistakably the critical and evaluating influence of conscious elaboration. Their immediate manifestation, as we encounter it in dreams and visions, is much more individual, less understandable, and more naïve than in myths, for example. The archetype is essentially an unconscious content that is altered by becoming conscious and by being perceived, and it takes its colour from the individual consciousness in which it happens to appear.[8]

85   As the archetypes, like all numinous contents, are relatively autonomous, they cannot be integrated simply by rational means, but require a dialectical procedure, a real coming to terms with them, often conducted by the patient in dialogue form, so that, without knowing it, he puts into effect the alchemical definition of the *meditatio*: "an inner colloquy with one's good angel." Usually the process runs a dramatic course, with many ups and downs. It expresses itself in, or is accompanied by, dream symbols that are related to the "représentations collectives," which in the form of mythological motifs have portrayed psychic processes of transformation since the earliest times.

---

[8] One must, for the sake of accuracy, distinguish between "archetype" and "archetypal ideas." The archetype as such is a hypothetical and irrepresentable model, something like the "pattern of behaviour" in biology. Cf. "On the Nature of the Psyche," sec. 7.

I

PSYCHOLOGICAL ASPECTS OF THE MOTHER ARCHETYPE

[First published as a lecture, "Die psychologischen Aspekte des Mutterarchetypus," in *Eranos-Jahrbuch 1938*. Later revised and published in *Von den Wurzeln des Bewusstseins* (Zurich, 1954). The present translation is of the latter, but it is also based partially on a translation of the 1938 version by Cary F. Baynes and Ximena de Angulo, privately issued in *Spring* (New York), 1943.—EDITORS.]

1. ON THE CONCEPT OF THE ARCHETYPE

148   The concept of the Great Mother belongs to the field of comparative religion and embraces widely varying types of mother-goddess. The concept itself is of no immediate concern to psychology, because the image of a Great Mother in this form is rarely encountered in practice, and then only under very special conditions. The symbol is obviously a derivative of the *mother archetype*. If we venture to investigate the background of the Great Mother image from the standpoint of psychology, then the mother archetype, as the more inclusive of the two, must form the basis of our discussion. Though lengthy discussion of the *concept* of an archetype is hardly necessary at this stage, some preliminary remarks of a general nature may not be out of place.

149   In former times, despite some dissenting opinion and the influence of Aristotle, it was not too difficult to understand Plato's conception of the Idea as supraordinate and pre-existent to all phenomena. "Archetype," far from being a modern term, was already in use before the time of St. Augustine, and was synonymous with "Idea" in the Platonic usage. When the *Corpus Hermeticum,* which probably dates from the third century, describes God as τὸ ἀρχέτυπον φῶς, the 'archetypal light,' it expresses the idea that he is the prototype of all light; that is to say, pre-existent and supraordinate to the phenomenon "light." Were I a philosopher, I should continue in this Platonic strain and say: Somewhere, in "a place beyond the skies," there is a prototype or primordial image of the mother that is pre-existent and supraordinate to all phenomena in which the "maternal," in the broadest sense of the term, is manifest. But I am an empiricist, not a philosopher; I cannot let myself presuppose that my peculiar temperament, my own attitude to intellectual problems, is universally valid. Apparently this is an assumption in which only the philosopher may indulge, who always takes it for granted that his own disposition and attitude are universal,

9

and will not recognize the fact, if he can avoid it, that his "personal equation" conditions his philosophy. As an empiricist, I must point out that there is a temperament which regards ideas as real entities and not merely as *nomina*. It so happens—by the merest accident, one might say—that for the past two hundred years we have been living in an age in which it has become unpopular or even unintelligible to suppose that ideas could be anything but *nomina*. Anyone who continues to think as Plato did must pay for his anachronism by seeing the "supracelestial," i.e., metaphysical, essence of the Idea relegated to the unverifiable realm of faith and superstition, or charitably left to the poet. Once again, in the age-old controversy over universals, the nominalistic standpoint has triumphed over the realistic, and the Idea has evaporated into a mere *flatus vocis*. This change was accompanied—and, indeed, to a considerable degree caused—by the marked rise of empiricism, the advantages of which were only too obvious to the intellect. Since that time the Idea is no longer something *a priori*, but is secondary and derived. Naturally, the new nominalism promptly claimed universal validity for itself in spite of the fact that it, too, is based on a definite and limited thesis coloured by temperament. This thesis runs as follows: we accept as valid anything that comes from outside and can be verified. The ideal instance is verification by experiment. The antithesis is: we accept as valid anything that comes from inside and cannot be verified. The hopelessness of this position is obvious. Greek natural philosophy with its interest in matter, together with Aristotelian reasoning, has achieved a belated but overwhelming victory over Plato.

150   Yet every victory contains the germ of future defeat. In our own day signs foreshadowing a change of attitude are rapidly increasing. Significantly enough, it is Kant's doctrine of categories, more than anything else, that destroys in embryo every attempt to revive metaphysics in the old sense of the word, but at the same time paves the way for a rebirth of the Platonic spirit. If it be true that there can be no metaphysics transcending human reason, it is no less true that there can be no empirical knowledge that is not already caught and limited by the *a priori* structure of cognition. During the century and a half that have elapsed since the appearance of the *Critique of Pure Reason*, the conviction has gradually gained ground that thinking, under-

standing, and reasoning cannot be regarded as independent processes subject only to the eternal laws of logic, but that they are *psychic functions* co-ordinated with the personality and subordinate to it. We no longer ask, "Has this or that been seen, heard, handled, weighed, counted, thought, and found to be logical?" We ask instead, "*Who* saw, heard, or thought?" Beginning with "the personal equation" in the observation and measurement of minimal processes, this critical attitude has gone on to the creation of an empirical psychology such as no time before ours has known. Today we are convinced that in all fields of knowledge psychological premises exist which exert a decisive influence upon the choice of material, the method of investigation, the nature of the conclusions, and the formulation of hypotheses and theories. We have even come to believe that Kant's personality was a decisive conditioning factor of his *Critique of Pure Reason*. Not only our philosophers, but our own predilections in philosophy, and even what we are fond of calling our "best" truths are affected, if not dangerously undermined, by this recognition of a personal premise. All creative freedom, we cry out, is taken away from us! What? Can it be possible that a man only thinks or says or does what he himself *is*?

151   Provided that we do not again exaggerate and so fall a victim to unrestrained "psychologizing," it seems to me that the critical standpoint here defined is inescapable. It constitutes the essence, origin, and method of modern psychology. There *is* an *a priori* factor in all human activities, namely the inborn, preconscious and unconscious individual structure of the psyche. The preconscious psyche—for example, that of a new-born infant—is not an empty vessel into which, under favourable conditions, practically anything can be poured. On the contrary, it is a tremendously complicated, sharply defined individual entity which appears indeterminate to us only because we cannot see it directly. But the moment the first visible manifestations of psychic life begin to appear, one would have to be blind not to recognize their individual character, that is, the unique personality behind them. It is hardly possible to suppose that all these details come into being only at the moment in which they appear. When it is a case of morbid predispositions already present in the parents, we infer hereditary transmission through

11

the germ-plasm; it would not occur to us to regard epilepsy in the child of an epileptic mother as an unaccountable mutation. Again, we explain by heredity the gifts and talents which can be traced back through whole generations. We explain in the same way the reappearance of complicated instinctive actions in animals that have never set eyes on their parents and therefore could not possibly have been "taught" by them.

¹⁵² Nowadays we have to start with the hypothesis that, so far as predisposition is concerned, there is no essential difference between man and all other creatures. Like every animal, he possesses a preformed psyche which breeds true to his species and which, on closer examination, reveals distinct features traceable to family antecedents. We have not the slightest reason to suppose that there are certain human activities or functions that could be exempted from this rule. We are unable to form any idea of what those dispositions or aptitudes are which make instinctive actions in animals possible. And it is just as impossible for us to know the nature of the preconscious psychic disposition that enables a child to react in a human manner. We can only suppose that his behaviour results from patterns of functioning, which I have described as *images*. The term "image" is intended to express not only the form of the activity taking place, but the typical situation in which the activity is released.[1] These images are "primordial" images in so far as they are peculiar to whole species, and if they ever "originated" their origin must have coincided at least with the beginning of the species. They are the "human quality" of the human being, the specifically human form his activities take. This specific form is hereditary and is already present in the germ-plasm. The idea that it is not inherited but comes into being in every child anew would be just as preposterous as the primitive belief that the sun which rises in the morning is a different sun from that which set the evening before.

¹⁵³ Since everything psychic is preformed, this must also be true of the individual functions, especially those which derive directly from the unconscious predisposition. The most important of these is creative fantasy. In the products of fantasy the primordial images are made visible, and it is here that the concept of the archetype finds its specific application. I do not claim to

[1] Cf. my "Instinct and the Unconscious," par. 277.

have been the first to point out this fact. The honour belongs to Plato. The first investigator in the field of ethnology to draw attention to the widespread occurrence of certain "elementary ideas" was Adolf Bastian. Two later investigators, Hubert and Mauss,[2] followers of Dürkheim, speak of "categories" of the imagination. And it was no less an authority than Hermann Usener [3] who first recognized unconscious preformation under the guise of "unconscious thinking." If I have any share in these discoveries, it consists in my having shown that archetypes are not disseminated only by tradition, language, and migration, but that they can rearise spontaneously, at any time, at any place, and without any outside influence.

154 The far-reaching implications of this statement must not be overlooked. For it means that there are present in every psyche forms which are unconscious but nonetheless active—living dispositions, ideas in the Platonic sense, that preform and continually influence our thoughts and feelings and actions.

155 Again and again I encounter the mistaken notion that an archetype is determined in regard to its content, in other words that it is a kind of unconscious idea (if such an expression be admissible). It is necessary to point out once more that archetypes are not determined as regards their content, but only as regards their form and then only to a very limited degree. A primordial image is determined as to its content only when it has become conscious and is therefore filled out with the material of conscious experience. Its form, however, as I have explained elsewhere, might perhaps be compared to the axial system of a crystal, which, as it were, preforms the crystalline structure in the mother liquid, although it has no material existence of its own. This first appears according to the specific way in which the ions and molecules aggregate. The archetype in itself is empty and purely formal, nothing but a *facultas praeformandi*, a possibility of representation which is given *a priori*. The representations themselves are not inherited, only the forms, and in that respect they correspond in every way to the instincts, which are also determined in form only. The existence of the instincts can no more be proved than the existence of the archetypes, so long as they do not manifest them-

2 [Cf. the previous paper, "Concerning the Archetypes," par. 137, n. 25.—EDITORS.]
3 Usener, *Das Weihnachtsfest*, p. 3.

selves concretely. With regard to the definiteness of the form, our comparison with the crystal is illuminating inasmuch as the axial system determines only the stereometric structure but not the concrete form of the individual crystal. This may be either large or small, and it may vary endlessly by reason of the different size of its planes or by the growing together of two crystals. The only thing that remains constant is the axial system, or rather, the invariable geometric proportions underlying it. The same is true of the archetype. In principle, it can be named and has an invariable nucleus of meaning—but always only in principle, never as regards its concrete manifestation. In the same way, the specific appearance of the mother-image at any given time cannot be deduced from the mother archetype alone, but depends on innumerable other factors.

2. THE MOTHER ARCHETYPE

156   Like any other archetype, the mother archetype appears under an almost infinite variety of aspects. I mention here only some of the more characteristic. First in importance are the personal mother and grandmother, stepmother and mother-in-law; then any woman with whom a relationship exists—for example, a nurse or governess or perhaps a remote ancestress. Then there are what might be termed mothers in a figurative sense. To this category belongs the goddess, and especially the Mother of God, the Virgin, and Sophia. Mythology offers many variations of the mother archetype, as for instance the mother who reappears as the maiden in the myth of Demeter and Kore; or the mother who is also the beloved, as in the Cybele-Attis myth. Other symbols of the mother in a figurative sense appear in things representing the goal of our longing for redemption, such as Paradise, the Kingdom of God, the Heavenly Jerusalem. Many things arousing devotion or feelings of awe, as for instance the Church, university, city or country, heaven, earth, the woods, the sea or any still waters, matter even, the underworld and the moon, can be mother-symbols. The archetype is often associated with things and places standing for fertility and fruitfulness: the cornucopia, a ploughed field, a garden. It can be attached to a rock, a cave, a tree, a spring, a deep well, or to various vessels such as the baptismal font, or to vessel-shaped flowers like the rose or the lotus. Because of the protection it implies, the magic circle or mandala can be a form of mother archetype. Hollow objects such as ovens and cooking vessels are associated with the mother archetype, and, of course, the uterus, *yoni*, and anything of a like shape. Added to this list there are many animals, such as the cow, hare, and helpful animals in general.

157   All these symbols can have a positive, favourable meaning or a negative, evil meaning. An ambivalent aspect is seen in the goddesses of fate (Moira, Graeae, Norns). Evil symbols are the

witch, the dragon (or any devouring and entwining animal, such as a large fish or a serpent), the grave, the sarcophagus, deep water, death, nightmares and bogies (Empusa, Lilith, etc.). This list is not, of course, complete; it presents only the most important features of the mother archetype.

158   The qualities associated with it are maternal solicitude and sympathy; the magic authority of the female; the wisdom and spiritual exaltation that transcend reason; any helpful instinct or impulse; all that is benign, all that cherishes and sustains, that fosters growth and fertility. The place of magic transformation and rebirth, together with the underworld and its inhabitants, are presided over by the mother. On the negative side the mother archetype may connote anything secret, hidden, dark; the abyss, the world of the dead, anything that devours, seduces, and poisons, that is terrifying and inescapable like fate. All these attributes of the mother archetype have been fully described and documented in my book *Symbols of Transformation*. There I formulated the ambivalence of these attributes as "the loving and the terrible mother." Perhaps the historical example of the dual nature of the mother most familiar to us is the Virgin Mary, who is not only the Lord's mother, but also, according to the medieval allegories, his cross. In India, "the loving and terrible mother" is the paradoxical Kali. Sankhya philosophy has elaborated the mother archetype into the concept of *prakṛti* (matter) and assigned to it the three *gunas* or fundamental attributes: *sattva, rajas, tamas:* goodness, passion, and darkness.[1] These are three essential aspects of the mother: her cherishing and nourishing goodness, her orgiastic emotionality, and her Stygian depths. The special feature of the philosophical myth, which shows Prakṛti dancing before Purusha in order to remind him of "discriminating knowledge," does not belong to the mother archetype but to the archetype of the anima, which in a man's psychology invariably appears, at first, mingled with the mother-image.

159   Although the figure of the mother as it appears in folklore is more or less universal, this image changes markedly when it appears in the individual psyche. In treating patients one is at

---

[1] This is the etymological meaning of the three *gunas*. See Weckerling, *Ananda-raya-makhi: Das Glück des Lebens*, pp. 21ff., and Garbe, *Die Samkhya Philosophie*, pp. 272ff. [Cf. also Zimmer, *Philosophies of India*, index, s.v.—EDITORS.]

first impressed, and indeed arrested, by the apparent significance of the personal mother. This figure of the personal mother looms so large in all personalistic psychologies that, as we know, they never got beyond it, even in theory, to other important aetiological factors. My own view differs from that of other medico-psychological theories principally in that I attribute to the personal mother only a limited aetiological significance. That is to say, all those influences which the literature describes as being exerted on the children do not come from the mother herself, but rather from the archetype projected upon her, which gives her a mythological background and invests her with authority and numinosity.[2] The aetiological and traumatic effects produced by the mother must be divided into two groups: (1) those corresponding to traits of character or attitudes actually present in the mother, and (2) those referring to traits which the mother only seems to possess, the reality being composed of more or less fantastic (i.e., archetypal) projections on the part of the child. Freud himself had already seen that the real aetiology of neuroses does not lie in traumatic effects, as he at first suspected, but in a peculiar development of infantile fantasy. This is not to deny that such a development can be traced back to disturbing influences emanating from the mother. I myself make it a rule to look first for the cause of infantile neuroses in the mother, as I know from experience that a child is much more likely to develop normally than neurotically, and that in the great majority of cases definite causes of disturbances can be found in the parents, especially in the mother. The contents of the child's abnormal fantasies can be referred to the personal mother only in part, since they often contain clear and unmistakable allusions which could not possibly have reference to human beings. This is especially true where definitely mythological products are concerned, as is frequently the case in infantile phobias where the mother may appear as a wild beast, a witch, a spectre, an ogre, a hermaphrodite, and so on. It must be borne in mind, however, that such fantasies are not always of unmistakably mythological origin, and even if they are, they may not always be rooted in the unconscious archetype but may have been occasioned by fairytales or accidental remarks. A

2 American psychology can supply us with any amount of examples. A blistering but instructive lampoon on this subject is Philip Wylie's *Generation of Vipers*.

thorough investigation is therefore indicated in each case. For practical reasons, such an investigation cannot be made so readily with children as with adults, who almost invariably transfer their fantasies to the physician during treatment—or, to be more precise, the fantasies are projected upon him automatically.

160   When that happens, nothing is gained by brushing them aside as ridiculous, for archetypes are among the inalienable assets of every psyche. They form the "treasure in the realm of shadowy thoughts" of which Kant spoke, and of which we have ample evidence in the countless treasure motifs of mythology. An archetype is in no sense just an annoying prejudice; it becomes so only when it is in the wrong place. In themselves, archetypal images are among the highest values of the human psyche; they have peopled the heavens of all races from time immemorial. To discard them as valueless would be a distinct loss. Our task is not, therefore, to deny the archetype, but to dissolve the projections, in order to restore their contents to the individual who has involuntarily lost them by projecting them outside himself.

3. THE MOTHER-COMPLEX

161   The mother archetype forms the foundation of the so-called mother-complex. It is an open question whether a mother-complex can develop without the mother having taken part in its formation as a demonstrable causal factor. My own experience leads me to believe that the mother always plays an active part in the origin of the disturbance, especially in infantile neuroses or in neuroses whose aetiology undoubtedly dates back to early childhood. In any event, the child's instincts are disturbed, and this constellates archetypes which, in their turn, produce fantasies that come between the child and its mother as an alien and often frightening element. Thus, if the children of an overanxious mother regularly dream that she is a terrifying animal or a witch, these experiences point to a split in the child's psyche that predisposes it to a neurosis.

I. THE MOTHER-COMPLEX OF THE SON

162   The effects of the mother-complex differ according to whether it appears in a son or a daughter. Typical effects on the son are homosexuality and Don Juanism, and sometimes also impotence.[1] In homosexuality, the son's entire heterosexuality is tied to the mother in an unconscious form; in Don Juanism, he unconsciously seeks his mother in every woman he meets. The effects of a mother-complex on the son may be seen in the ideology of the Cybele and Attis type: self-castration, madness, and early death. Because of the difference in sex, a son's mother-complex does not appear in pure form. This is the reason why in every masculine mother-complex, side by side with the mother archetype, a significant role is played by the image of the man's sexual counterpart, the anima. The mother is the first feminine being with whom the man-to-be comes in contact, and

1 But the father-complex also plays a considerable part here.

19

she cannot help playing, overtly or covertly, consciously or unconsciously, upon the son's masculinity, just as the son in his turn grows increasingly aware of his mother's femininity, or unconsciously responds to it by instinct. In the case of the son, therefore, the simple relationships of identity or of resistance and differentiation are continually cut across by erotic attraction or repulsion, which complicates matters very considerably. I do not mean to say that for this reason the mother-complex of a son ought to be regarded as more serious than that of a daughter. The investigation of these complex psychic phenomena is still in the pioneer stage. Comparisons will not become feasible until we have some statistics at our disposal, and of these, so far, there is no sign.

163   Only in the daughter is the mother-complex clear and uncomplicated. Here we have to do either with an overdevelopment of feminine instincts indirectly caused by the mother, or with a weakening of them to the point of complete extinction. In the first case, the preponderance of instinct makes the daughter unconscious of her own personality; in the latter, the instincts are projected upon the mother. For the present we must content ourselves with the statement that in the daughter a mother-complex either unduly stimulates or else inhibits the feminine instinct, and that in the son it injures the masculine instinct through an unnatural sexualization.

164   Since a "mother-complex" is a concept borrowed from psychopathology, it is always associated with the idea of injury and illness. But if we take the concept out of its narrow psychopathological setting and give it a wider connotation, we can see that it has positive effects as well. Thus a man with a mother-complex may have a finely differentiated Eros [2] instead of, or in addition to, homosexuality. (Something of this sort is suggested by Plato in his *Symposium*.) This gives him a great capacity for friendship, which often creates ties of astonishing tenderness between men and may even rescue friendship between the sexes from the limbo of the impossible. He may have good taste and an aesthetic sense which are fostered by the presence of a feminine streak. Then he may be supremely gifted as a teacher because of his almost feminine insight and tact. He is likely to have a feeling for history, and to be conservative in the best

2 [Cf. *Two Essays on Analytical Psychology*, pars. 16ff.—EDITORS.]

sense and cherish the values of the past. Often he is endowed with a wealth of religious feelings, which help to bring the *ecclesia spiritualis* into reality; and a spiritual receptivity which makes him responsive to revelation.

165   In the same way, what in its negative aspect is Don Juanism can appear positively as bold and resolute manliness; ambitious striving after the highest goals; opposition to all stupidity, narrow-mindedness, injustice, and laziness; willingness to make sacrifices for what is regarded as right, sometimes bordering on heroism; perseverance, inflexibility and toughness of will; a curiosity that does not shrink even from the riddles of the universe; and finally, a revolutionary spirit which strives to put a new face upon the world.

166   All these possibilities are reflected in the mythological motifs enumerated earlier as different aspects of the mother archetype. As I have already dealt with the mother-complex of the son, including the anima complication, elsewhere, and my present theme is the archetype of the mother, in the following discussion I shall relegate masculine psychology to the background.

II. THE MOTHER-COMPLEX OF THE DAUGHTER [3]

167   (a) *Hypertrophy of the Maternal Element.*—We have noted that in the daughter the mother-complex leads either to a hypertrophy of the feminine side or to its atrophy. The exaggeration of the feminine side means an intensification of all female instincts, above all the maternal instinct. The negative aspect is seen in the woman whose only goal is childbirth. To her the husband is obviously of secondary importance; he is first and foremost the instrument of procreation, and she regards him merely as an object to be looked after, along with children, poor relations, cats, dogs, and household furniture. Even her own

[3] In the present section I propose to present a series of different "types" of mother-complex; in formulating them, I am drawing on my own therapeutic experiences. "Types" are not individual cases, neither are they freely invented schemata into which all individual cases have to be fitted. "Types" are ideal instances, or pictures of the average run of experience, with which no single individual can be identified. People whose experience is confined to books or psychological laboratories can form no proper idea of the cumulative experience of a practising psychologist.

personality is of secondary importance; she often remains entirely unconscious of it, for her life is lived in and through others, in more or less complete identification with all the objects of her care. First she gives birth to the children, and from then on she clings to them, for without them she has no existence whatsoever. Like Demeter, she compels the gods by her stubborn persistence to grant her the right of possession over her daughter. Her Eros develops exclusively as a maternal relationship while remaining unconscious as a personal one. An unconscious Eros always expresses itself as will to power.[4] Women of this type, though continually "living for others," are, as a matter of fact, unable to make any real sacrifice. Driven by ruthless will to power and a fanatical insistence on their own maternal rights, they often succeed in annihilating not only their own personality but also the personal lives of their children. The less conscious such a mother is of her own personality, the greater and the more violent is her unconscious will to power. For many such women Baubo rather than Demeter would be the appropriate symbol. The mind is not cultivated for its own sake but usually remains in its original condition, altogether primitive, unrelated, and ruthless, but also as true, and sometimes as profound, as Nature herself.[5] She herself does not know this and is therefore unable to appreciate the wittiness of her mind or to marvel philosophically at its profundity; like as not she will immediately forget what she has said.

168   (b) *Overdevelopment of Eros.*—It by no means follows that the complex induced in a daughter by such a mother must necessarily result in hypertrophy of the maternal instinct. Quite the contrary, this instinct may be wiped out altogether. As a substitute, an overdeveloped Eros results, and this almost invariably leads to an unconscious incestuous relationship with the father.[6] The intensified Eros places an abnormal emphasis on the personality of others. Jealousy of the mother and the desire to outdo her become the leitmotifs of subsequent undertakings, which

4 This statement is based on the repeated experience that, where love is lacking, power fills the vacuum.

5 In my English seminars [privately distributed] I have called this the "natural mind."

6 Here the initiative comes from the daughter. In other cases the father's psychology is responsible; his projection of the anima arouses an incestuous fixation in the daughter.

are often disastrous. A woman of this type loves romantic and sensational episodes for their own sake, and is interested in married men, less for themselves than for the fact that they are married and so give her an opportunity to wreck a marriage, that being the whole point of her manoeuvre. Once the goal is attained, her interest evaporates for lack of any maternal instinct, and then it will be someone else's turn.[7] This type is noted for its remarkable unconsciousness. Such women really seem to be utterly blind to what they are doing,[8] which is anything but advantageous either for themselves or for their victims. I need hardly point out that for men with a passive Eros this type offers an excellent hook for anima projections.

169   (c) *Identity with the Mother.*—If a mother-complex in a woman does not produce an overdeveloped Eros, it leads to identification with the mother and to paralysis of the daughter's feminine initiative. A complete projection of her personality on to the mother then takes place, owing to the fact that she is unconscious both of her maternal instinct and of her Eros. Everything which reminds her of motherhood, responsibility, personal relationships, and erotic demands arouses feelings of inferiority and compels her to run away—to her mother, naturally, who lives to perfection everything that seems unattainable to her daughter. As a sort of superwoman (admired involuntarily by the daughter), the mother lives out for her beforehand all that the girl might have lived for herself. She is content to cling to her mother in selfless devotion, while at the same time unconsciously striving, almost against her will, to tyrannize over her, naturally under the mask of complete loyalty and devotion. The daughter leads a shadow-existence, often visibly sucked dry by her mother, and she prolongs her mother's life by a sort of continuous blood transfusion. These bloodless maidens are by no means immune to marriage. On the contrary, despite their shadowiness and passivity, they command a high price on the marriage market. First, they are so empty that a man is free to impute to them anything he fancies. In addition, they are so unconscious that the unconscious puts out countless invisible

---

7 Herein lies the difference between this type of complex and the feminine father-complex related to it, where the "father" is mothered and coddled.
8 This does not mean that they are unconscious of the *facts.* It is only their *meaning* that escapes them.

feelers, veritable octopus-tentacles, that suck up all masculine projections; and this pleases men enormously. All that feminine indefiniteness is the longed-for counterpart of male decisiveness and single-mindedness, which can be satisfactorily achieved only if a man can get rid of everything doubtful, ambiguous, vague, and muddled by projecting it upon some charming example of feminine innocence.[9] Because of the woman's characteristic passivity, and the feelings of inferiority which make her continually play the injured innocent, the man finds himself cast in an attractive role: he has the privilege of putting up with the familiar feminine foibles with real superiority, and yet with forbearance, like a true knight. (Fortunately, he remains ignorant of the fact that these deficiencies consist largely of his own projections.) The girl's notorious helplessness is a special attraction. She is so much an appendage of her mother that she can only flutter confusedly when a man approaches. She just doesn't know a thing. She is so inexperienced, so terribly in need of help, that even the gentlest swain becomes a daring abductor who brutally robs a loving mother of her daughter. Such a marvellous opportunity to pass himself off as a gay Lothario does not occur every day and therefore acts as a strong incentive. This was how Pluto abducted Persephone from the inconsolable Demeter. But, by a decree of the gods, he had to surrender his wife every year to his mother-in-law for the summer season. (The attentive reader will note that such legends do not come about by chance!)

170   (d) *Resistance to the Mother.*—These three extreme types are linked together by many intermediate stages, of which I shall mention only one important example. In the particular intermediate type I have in mind, the problem is less an over-development or an inhibition of the feminine instincts than an overwhelming resistance to maternal supremacy, often to the exclusion of all else. It is the supreme example of the negative mother-complex. The motto of this type is: Anything, so long as it is not like Mother! On one hand we have a fascination which never reaches the point of identification; on the other, an intensification of Eros which exhausts itself in jealous resist-

[9] This type of woman has an oddly disarming effect on her husband, but only until he discovers that the person he has married and who shares his nuptial bed is his mother-in-law.

ance. This kind of daughter knows what she does *not* want, but is usually completely at sea as to what she would choose as her own fate. All her instincts are concentrated on the mother in the negative form of resistance and are therefore of no use to her in building her own life. Should she get as far as marrying, either the marriage will be used for the sole purpose of escaping from her mother, or else a diabolical fate will present her with a husband who shares all the essential traits of her mother's character. All instinctive processes meet with unexpected difficulties; either sexuality does not function properly, or the children are unwanted, or maternal duties seem unbearable, or the demands of marital life are responded to with impatience and irritation. This is quite natural, since none of it has anything to do with the realities of life when stubborn resistance to the power of the mother in every form has come to be life's dominating aim. In such cases one can often see the attributes of the mother archetype demonstrated in every detail. For example, the mother as representative of the family (or clan) causes either violent resistances or complete indifference to anything that comes under the head of family, community, society, convention, and the like. Resistance to the mother as *uterus* often manifests itself in menstrual disturbances, failure of conception, abhorrence of pregnancy, hemorrhages and excessive vomiting during pregnancy, miscarriages, and so on. The mother as *materia*, 'matter,' may be at the back of these women's impatience with objects, their clumsy handling of tools and crockery and bad taste in clothes.

171   Again, resistance to the mother can sometimes result in a spontaneous development of intellect for the purpose of creating a sphere of interest in which the mother has no place. This development springs from the daughter's own needs and not at all for the sake of a man whom she would like to impress or dazzle by a semblance of intellectual comradeship. Its real purpose is to break the mother's power by intellectual criticism and superior knowledge, so as to enumerate to her all her stupidities, mistakes in logic, and educational shortcomings. Intellectual development is often accompanied by the emergence of masculine traits in general.

4. POSITIVE ASPECTS OF THE
MOTHER-COMPLEX

I. THE MOTHER

¹⁷² The positive aspect of the first type of complex, namely the overdevelopment of the maternal instinct, is identical with that well-known image of the mother which has been glorified in all ages and all tongues. This is the mother-love which is one of the most moving and unforgettable memories of our lives, the mysterious root of all growth and change; the love that means homecoming, shelter, and the long silence from which everything begins and in which everything ends. Intimately known and yet strange like Nature, lovingly tender and yet cruel like fate, joyous and untiring giver of life—*mater dolorosa* and mute implacable portal that closes upon the dead. Mother is mother-love, *my* experience and *my* secret. Why risk saying too much, too much that is false and inadequate and beside the point, about that human being who was our mother, the accidental carrier of that great experience which includes herself and myself and all mankind, and indeed the whole of created nature, the experience of life whose children we are? The attempt to say these things has always been made, and probably always will be; but a sensitive person cannot in all fairness load that enormous burden of meaning, responsibility, duty, heaven and hell, on to the shoulders of one frail and fallible human being—so deserving of love, indulgence, understanding, and forgiveness—who was our mother. He knows that the mother carries for us that inborn image of the *mater natura* and *mater spiritualis,* of the totality of life of which we are a small and helpless part. Nor should we hesitate for one moment to relieve the human mother of this appalling burden, for our own sakes as well as hers. It is just this massive weight of meaning that ties us to the mother and chains her to her child, to the physical and mental

26

detriment of both. A mother-complex is not got rid of by blindly reducing the mother to human proportions. Besides that we run the risk of dissolving the experience "Mother" into atoms, thus destroying something supremely valuable and throwing away the golden key which a good fairy laid in our cradle. That is why mankind has always instinctively added the pre-existent divine pair to the personal parents—the "god"-father and "god"-mother of the newborn child—so that, from sheer unconsciousness or shortsighted rationalism, he should never forget himself so far as to invest his own parents with divinity.

173   The archetype is really far less a scientific problem than an urgent question of psychic hygiene. Even if all proofs of the existence of archetypes were lacking, and all the clever people in the world succeeded in convincing us that such a thing could not possibly exist, we would have to invent them forthwith in order to keep our highest and most important values from disappearing into the unconscious. For when these fall into the unconscious the whole elemental force of the original experience is lost. What then appears in its place is fixation on the mother-imago; and when this has been sufficiently rationalized and "corrected," we are tied fast to human reason and condemned from then on to believe exclusively in what is rational. That is a virtue and an advantage on the one hand, but on the other a limitation and impoverishment, for it brings us nearer to the bleakness of doctrinairism and "enlightenment." This Déesse Raison emits a deceptive light which illuminates only what we know already, but spreads a darkness over all those things which it would be most needful for us to know and become conscious of. The more independent "reason" pretends to be, the more it turns into sheer intellectuality which puts doctrine in the place of reality and shows us man not as he is but how it wants him to be.

174   Whether he understands them or not, man must remain conscious of the world of the archetypes, because in it he is still a part of Nature and is connected with his own roots. A view of the world or a social order that cuts him off from the primordial images of life not only is no culture at all but, in increasing degree, is a prison or a stable. If the primordial images remain conscious in some form or other, the energy that belongs to

them can flow freely into man. But when it is no longer possible to maintain contact with them, then the tremendous sum of energy stored up in these images, which is also the source of the fascination underlying the infantile parental complex, falls back into the unconscious. The unconscious then becomes charged with a force that acts as an irresistible *vis a tergo* to whatever view or idea or tendency our intellect may choose to dangle enticingly before our desiring eyes. In this way man is delivered over to his conscious side, and reason becomes the arbiter of right and wrong, of good and evil. I am far from wishing to belittle the divine gift of reason, man's highest faculty. But in the role of absolute tyrant it has no meaning—no more than light would have in a world where its counterpart, darkness, was absent. Man would do well to heed the wise counsel of the mother and obey the inexorable law of nature which sets limits to every being. He ought never to forget that the world exists only because opposing forces are held in equilibrium. So, too, the rational is counterbalanced by the irrational, and what is planned and purposed by what *is*.

175   This excursion into the realm of generalities was unavoidable, because the mother is the first world of the child and the last world of the adult. We are all wrapped as her children in the mantle of this great Isis. But let us now return to the different types of feminine mother-complex. It may seem strange that I am devoting so much more time to the mother-complex in woman than to its counterpart in man. The reason for this has already been mentioned: in a man, the mother-complex is never "pure," it is always mixed with the anima archetype, and the consequence is that a man's statements about the mother are always emotionally prejudiced in the sense of showing "animosity." Only in women is it possible to examine the effects of the mother archetype without admixture of animosity, and even this has prospects of success only when no compensating animus has developed.

II. THE OVERDEVELOPED EROS

176   I drew a very unfavourable picture of this type as we encounter it in the field of psychopathology. But this type, uninviting

as it appears, also has positive aspects which society could ill afford to do without. Indeed, behind what is possibly the worst effect of this attitude, the unscrupulous wrecking of marriages, we can see an extremely significant and purposeful arrangement of nature. This type often develops in reaction to a mother who is wholly a thrall of nature, purely instinctive and therefore all-devouring. Such a mother is an anachronism, a throw-back to a primitive state of matriarchy where the man leads an insipid existence as a mere procreator and serf of the soil. The reactive intensification of the daughter's Eros is aimed at some man who ought to be rescued from the preponderance of the female-maternal element in his life. A woman of this type instinctively intervenes when provoked by the unconsciousness of the marriage partner. She will disturb that comfortable ease so danger-ous to the personality of a man but frequently regarded by him as marital faithfulness. This complacency leads to blank uncon-sciousness of his own personality and to those supposedly ideal marriages where he is nothing but Dad and she is nothing but Mom, and they even call each other that. This is a slippery path that can easily degrade marriage to the level of a mere breeding-pen.

177   A woman of this type directs the burning ray of her Eros upon a man whose life is stifled by maternal solicitude, and by doing so she arouses a moral conflict. Yet without this there can be no consciousness of personality. "But why on earth," you may ask, "should it be necessary for man to achieve, by hook or by crook, a higher level of consciousness?" This is truly the cru-cial question, and I do not find the answer easy. Instead of a real answer I can only make a confession of faith: I believe that, after thousands and millions of years, someone had to realize that this wonderful world of mountains and oceans, suns and moons, galaxies and nebulae, plants and animals, *exists*. From a low hill in the Athi plains of East Africa I once watched the vast herds of wild animals grazing in soundless stillness, as they had done from time immemorial, touched only by the breath of a primeval world. I felt then as if I were the first man, the first creature, to know that all this *is*. The entire world round me was still in its primeval state; it did not know that it *was*. And then, in that one moment in which I came to know, the world sprang into being; without that moment it would never have

been. All Nature seeks this goal and finds it fulfilled in man, but only in the most highly developed and most fully conscious man. Every advance, even the smallest, along this path of conscious realization adds that much to the world.

178 There is no consciousness without discrimination of opposites. This is the paternal principle, the Logos, which eternally struggles to extricate itself from the primal warmth and primal darkness of the maternal womb; in a word, from unconsciousness. Divine curiosity yearns to be born and does not shrink from conflict, suffering, or sin. Unconsciousness is the primal sin, evil itself, for the Logos. Therefore its first creative act of liberation is matricide, and the spirit that dared all heights and all depths must, as Synesius says, suffer the divine punishment, enchainment on the rocks of the Caucasus. Nothing can exist without its opposite; the two were one in the beginning and will be one again in the end. Consciousness can only exist through continual recognition of the unconscious, just as everything that lives must pass through many deaths.

179 The stirring up of conflict is a Luciferian virtue in the true sense of the word. Conflict engenders fire, the fire of affects and emotions, and like every other fire it has two aspects, that of combustion and that of creating light. On the one hand, emotion is the alchemical fire whose warmth brings everything into existence and whose heat burns all superfluities to ashes (*omnes superfluitates comburit*). But on the other hand, emotion is the moment when steel meets flint and a spark is struck forth, for emotion is the chief source of consciousness. There is no change from darkness to light or from inertia to movement without emotion.

180 The woman whose fate it is to be a disturbing element is not solely destructive, except in pathological cases. Normally the disturber is herself caught in the disturbance; the worker of change is herself changed, and the glare of the fire she ignites both illuminates and enlightens all the victims of the entanglement. What seemed a senseless upheaval becomes a process of purification:

> So that all that is vain
> Might dwindle and wane.[1]

1 *Faust*, Part II, Act 5.

181   If a woman of this type remains unconscious of the meaning of her function, if she does not know that she is

> Part of that power which would
> Ever work evil but engenders good,[2]

she will herself perish by the sword she brings. But consciousness transforms her into a deliverer and redeemer.

III. THE "NOTHING-BUT" DAUGHTER

182   The woman of the third type, who is so identified with the mother that her own instincts are paralysed through projection, need not on that account remain a hopeless nonentity forever. On the contrary, if she is at all normal, there is a good chance of the empty vessel being filled by a potent anima projection. Indeed, the fate of such a woman depends on this eventuality; she can never find herself at all, not even approximately, without a man's help; she has to be literally abducted or stolen from her mother. Moreover, she must play the role mapped out for her for a long time and with great effort, until she actually comes to loathe it. In this way she may perhaps discover who she really is. Such women may become devoted and self-sacrificing wives of husbands whose whole existence turns on their identification with a profession or a great talent, but who, for the rest, are unconscious and remain so. Since they are nothing but masks themselves, the wife, too, must be able to play the accompanying part with a semblance of naturalness. But these women sometimes have valuable gifts which remained undeveloped only because they were entirely unconscious of their own personality. They may project the gift or talent upon a husband who lacks it himself, and then we have the spectacle of a totally insignificant man who seemed to have no chance whatsoever suddenly soaring as if on a magic carpet to the highest summits of achievement. *Cherchez la femme,* and you have the secret of his success. These women remind me—if I may be forgiven the impolite comparison—of hefty great bitches who turn tail before the smallest cur simply because he is a terrible male and it never occurs to them to bite him.

2 Ibid., Part I, Act 1.

183   Finally, it should be remarked that *emptiness* is a great feminine secret. It is something absolutely alien to man; the chasm, the unplumbed depths, the *yin*. The pitifulness of this vacuous nonentity goes to his heart (I speak here as a man), and one is tempted to say that this constitutes the whole "mystery" of woman. Such a female is fate itself. A man may say what he likes about it; be for it or against it, or both at once; in the end he falls, absurdly happy, into this pit, or, if he doesn't, he has missed and bungled his only chance of making a man of himself. In the first case one cannot disprove his foolish good luck to him, and in the second one cannot make his misfortune seem plausible. "The Mothers, the Mothers, how eerily it sounds!" [3] With this sigh, which seals the capitulation of the male as he approaches the realm of the Mothers, we will turn to the fourth type.

IV. THE NEGATIVE MOTHER-COMPLEX

184   As a pathological phenomenon this type is an unpleasant, exacting, and anything but satisfactory partner for her husband, since she rebels in every fibre of her being against everything that springs from natural soil. However, there is no reason why increasing experience of life should not teach her a thing or two, so that for a start she gives up fighting the mother in the personal and restricted sense. But even at her best she will remain hostile to all that is dark, unclear, and ambiguous, and will cultivate and emphasize everything certain and clear and reasonable. Excelling her more feminine sister in her objectivity and coolness of judgment, she may become the friend, sister, and competent adviser of her husband. Her own masculine aspirations make it possible for her to have a human understanding of the individuality of her husband quite transcending the realm of the erotic. The woman with this type of mother-complex probably has the best chance of all to make her marriage an outstanding success during the second half of life. But this is true only if she succeeds in overcoming the hell of "nothing but femininity," the chaos of the maternal womb, which is her greatest danger because of her negative complex. As we know, a com-

[3] Ibid., Part II, Act 1.

plex can be really overcome only if it is lived out to the full. In other words, if we are to develop further we have to draw to us and drink down to the very dregs what, because of our complexes, we have held at a distance.

185   This type started out in the world with averted face, like Lot's wife looking back on Sodom and Gomorrha. And all the while the world and life pass by her like a dream—an annoying source of illusions, disappointments, and irritations, all of which are due solely to the fact that she cannot bring herself to look straight ahead for once. Because of her merely unconscious, reactive attitude toward reality, her life actually becomes dominated by what she fought hardest against—the exclusively maternal feminine aspect. But if she should later turn her face, she will see the world for the first time, so to speak, in the light of maturity, and see it embellished with all the colours and enchanting wonders of youth, and sometimes even of childhood. It is a vision that brings knowledge and discovery of truth, the indispensable prerequisite for consciousness. A part of life was lost, but the meaning of life has been salvaged for her.

186   The woman who fights against her father still has the possibility of leading an instinctive, feminine existence, because she rejects only what is alien to her. But when she fights against the mother she may, at the risk of injury to her instincts, attain to greater consciousness, because in repudiating the mother she repudiates all that is obscure, instinctive, ambiguous, and unconscious in her own nature. Thanks to her lucidity, objectivity, and masculinity, a woman of this type is frequently found in important positions in which her tardily discovered maternal quality, guided by a cool intelligence, exerts a most beneficial influence. This rare combination of womanliness and masculine understanding proves valuable in the realm of intimate relationships as well as in practical matters. As the spiritual guide and adviser of a man, such a woman, unknown to the world, may play a highly influential part. Owing to her qualities, the masculine mind finds this type easier to understand than women with other forms of mother-complex, and for this reason men often favour her with the projection of positive mother-complexes. The excessively feminine woman terrifies men who have a mother-complex characterized by great sensitivity. But this woman is not frightening to a man, because she builds bridges

for the masculine mind over which he can safely guide his feelings to the opposite shore. Her clarity of understanding inspires him with confidence, a factor not to be underrated and one that is absent from the relationship between a man and a woman much more often than one might think. The man's Eros does not lead upward only but downward into that uncanny dark world of Hecate and Kali, which is a horror to any intellectual man. The understanding possessed by this type of woman will be a guiding star to him in the darkness and seemingly unending mazes of life.

5. CONCLUSION

187   From what has been said it should be clear that in the last analysis all the statements of mythology on this subject as well as the observed effects of the mother-complex, when stripped of their confusing detail, point to the unconscious as their place of origin. How else could it have occurred to man to divide the cosmos, on the analogy of day and night, summer and winter, into a bright day-world and a dark night-world peopled with fabulous monsters, unless he had the prototype of such a division in himself, in the polarity between the conscious and the invisible and unknowable unconscious? Primitive man's perception of objects is conditioned only partly by the objective behaviour of the things themselves, whereas a much greater part is often played by intrapsychic facts which are not related to the external objects except by way of projection.[1] This is due to the simple fact that the primitive has not yet experienced that ascetic discipline of mind known to us as the critique of knowledge. To him the world is a more or less fluid phenomenon within the stream of his own fantasy, where subject and object are undifferentiated and in a state of mutual interpenetration. "All that is outside, also is inside," we could say with Goethe. But this "inside," which modern rationalism is so eager to derive from "outside," has an *a priori* structure of its own that antedates all conscious experience. It is quite impossible to conceive how "experience" in the widest sense, or, for that matter, anything psychic, could originate exclusively in the outside world. The psyche is part of the inmost mystery of life, and it has its own peculiar structure and form like every other organism. Whether this psychic structure and its elements, the archetypes, ever "originated" at all is a metaphysical question and therefore unanswerable. The structure is something given, the precondition that is found to be present in every case. And this is the *mother*, the matrix—the form into which all experience is

1 [Cf. above, "Archetypes of the Collective Unconscious," par. 7.—EDITORS.]

poured. The *father*, on the other hand, represents the *dynamism* of the archetype, for the archetype consists of both—form and energy.

188   The carrier of the archetype is in the first place the personal mother, because the child lives at first in complete participation with her, in a state of unconscious identity. She is the psychic as well as the physical precondition of the child. With the awakening of ego-consciousness the participation gradually weakens, and consciousness begins to enter into opposition to the unconscious, its own precondition. This leads to differentiation of the ego from the mother, whose personal peculiarities gradually become more distinct. All the fabulous and mysterious qualities attaching to her image begin to fall away and are transferred to the person closest to her, for instance the grandmother. As the mother of the mother, she is "greater" than the latter; she is in truth the "grand" or "Great Mother." Not infrequently she assumes the attributes of wisdom as well as those of a witch. For the further the archetype recedes from consciousness and the clearer the latter becomes, the more distinctly does the archetype assume mythological features. The transition from mother to grandmother means that the archetype is elevated to a higher rank. This is clearly demonstrated in a notion held by the Bataks. The funeral sacrifice in honour of a dead father is modest, consisting of ordinary food. But if the son has a son of his own, then the father has become a grandfather and has consequently attained a more dignified status in the Beyond, and very important offerings are made to him.[2]

189   As the distance between conscious and unconscious increases, the grandmother's more exalted rank transforms her into a "Great Mother," and it frequently happens that the opposites contained in this image split apart. We then get a good fairy and a wicked fairy, or a benevolent goddess and one who is malevolent and dangerous. In Western antiquity and especially in Eastern cultures the opposites often remain united in the same figure, though this paradox does not disturb the primitive mind in the least. The legends about the gods are as full of contradictions as are their moral characters. In the West, the paradoxical behaviour and moral ambivalence of the gods scandalized people even in antiquity and gave rise to criticism that led

[2] Warnecke, *Die Religion der Batak*.

finally to a devaluation of the Olympians on the one hand and to their philosophical interpretation on the other. The clearest expression of this is the Christian reformation of the Jewish concept of the Deity: the morally ambiguous Yahweh became an exclusively good God, while everything evil was united in the devil. It seems as if the development of the feeling function in Western man forced a choice on him which led to the moral splitting of the divinity into two halves. In the East the predominantly intuitive intellectual attitude left no room for feeling values, and the gods—Kali is a case in point—could retain their original paradoxical morality undisturbed. Thus Kali is representative of the East and the Madonna of the West. The latter has entirely lost the shadow that still distantly followed her in the allegories of the Middle Ages. It was relegated to the hell of popular imagination, where it now leads an insignificant existence as the devil's grandmother.[3] Thanks to the development of feeling-values, the splendour of the "light" god has been enhanced beyond measure, but the darkness supposedly represented by the devil has localized itself in man. This strange development was precipitated chiefly by the fact that Christianity, terrified of Manichaean dualism, strove to preserve its monotheism by main force. But since the reality of darkness and evil could not be denied, there was no alternative but to make man responsible for it. Even the devil was largely, if not entirely, abolished, with the result that this metaphysical figure, who at one time was an integral part of the Deity, was introjected into man, who thereupon became the real carrier of the *mysterium iniquitatis*: "omne bonum a Deo, omne malum ab homine." In recent times this development has suffered a diabolical reverse, and the wolf in sheep's clothing now goes about whispering in our ear that evil is really nothing but a misunderstanding of good and an effective instrument of progress. We think that the world of darkness has thus been abolished for good and all, and nobody realizes what a poisoning this is of man's soul. In this way he turns himself into the devil, for the devil is half of the archetype whose irresistible power makes even unbelievers ejaculate "Oh God!" on every suitable and unsuitable occasion. If one can possibly avoid it, one ought never to identify with an archetype, for, as psychopathology

[3] [A familiar figure of speech in German.—EDITORS.]

and certain contemporary events show, the consequences are terrifying.

190 Western man has sunk to such a low level spiritually that he even has to deny the apotheosis of untamed and untameable psychic power—the divinity itself—so that, after swallowing evil, he may possess himself of the good as well. If you read Nietzsche's *Zarathustra* with attention and psychological understanding, you will see that he has described with rare consistency and with the passion of a truly religious person the psychology of the "Superman" for whom God is dead, and who is himself burst asunder because he tried to imprison the divine paradox within the narrow framework of the mortal man. Goethe has wisely said: "What terror then shall seize the Superman!"—and was rewarded with a supercilious smile from the Philistines. His glorification of the Mother who is great enough to include in herself both the Queen of Heaven and Maria Aegyptiaca is supreme wisdom and profoundly significant for anyone willing to reflect upon it. But what can one expect in an age when the official spokesmen of Christianity publicly announce their inability to understand the foundations of religious experience! I extract the following sentence from an article by a Protestant theologian: "We understand ourselves—whether naturalistically or idealistically—to be *homogeneous creatures who are not so peculiarly divided that alien forces can intervene in our inner life,* as the New Testament supposes." [4] (Italics mine.) The author is evidently unacquainted with the fact that science demonstrated the lability and dissociability of consciousness more than half a century ago and proved it by experiment. Our conscious intentions are continually disturbed and thwarted, to a greater or lesser degree, by unconscious intrusions whose causes are at first strange to us. The psyche is far from being a homogeneous unit—on the contrary, it is a boiling cauldron of contradictory impulses, inhibitions, and affects, and for many people the conflict between them is so insupportable that they even wish for the deliverance preached by theologians. Deliverance from what? Obviously, from a highly questionable psychic state. The unity of consciousness or of the so-called personality is not a reality at all but a desideratum. I still have a vivid memory of a certain philosopher who also raved about this unity and

4 Buri, "Theologie und Philosophie," p. 117. [Quoting Rudolf Bultmann.—EDS.]

used to consult me about his neurosis: he was obsessed by the idea that he was suffering from cancer. I do not know how many specialists he had consulted already, and how many X-ray pictures he had had made. They all assured him that he had no cancer. He himself told me: "I know I have no cancer, but I still could have one." Who is responsible for this "imaginary" idea? He certainly did not make it himself; it was forced on him by an "alien" power. There is little to choose between this state and that of the man possessed in the New Testament. Now whether you believe in a demon of the air or in a factor in the unconscious that plays diabolical tricks on you is all one to me. The fact that man's imagined unity is menaced by alien powers remains the same in either case. Theologians would do better to take account for once of these psychological facts than to go on "demythologizing" them with rationalistic explanations that are a hundred years behind the times.

*

191   I have tried in the foregoing to give a survey of the psychic phenomena that may be attributed to the predominance of the mother-image. Although I have not always drawn attention to them, my reader will presumably have had no difficulty in recognizing those features which characterize the Great Mother mythologically, even when they appear under the guise of personalistic psychology. When we ask patients who are particularly influenced by the mother-image to express in words or pictures what "Mother" means to them—be it positive or negative— we invariably get symbolical figures which must be regarded as direct analogies of the mythological mother-image. These analogies take us into a field that still requires a great deal more work of elucidation. At any rate, I personally do not feel able to say anything definitive about it. If, nevertheless, I venture to offer a few suggestions, they should be regarded as altogether provisional and tentative.

192   Above all, I should like to point out that the mother-image in a man's psychology is entirely different in character from a woman's. For a woman, the mother typifies her own conscious life as conditioned by her sex. But for a man the mother typifies something alien, which he has yet to experience and which is filled with the imagery latent in the unconscious. For this

reason, if for no other, the mother-image of a man is essentially different from a woman's. The mother has from the outset a decidedly symbolical significance for a man, which probably accounts for his strong tendency to idealize her. Idealization is a hidden apotropaism; one idealizes whenever there is a secret fear to be exorcized. What is feared is the unconscious and its magical influence.[5]

193   Whereas for a man the mother is *ipso facto* symbolical, for a woman she becomes a symbol only in the course of her psychological development. Experience reveals the striking fact that the Urania type of mother-image predominates in masculine psychology, whereas in a woman the chthonic type, or Earth Mother, is the most frequent. During the manifest phase of the archetype an almost complete identification takes place. A woman can identify directly with the Earth Mother, but a man cannot (except in psychotic cases). As mythology shows, one of the peculiarities of the Great Mother is that she frequently appears paired with her male counterpart. Accordingly the man identifies with the son-lover on whom the grace of Sophia has descended, with a *puer aeternus* or a *filius sapientiae*. But the companion of the chthonic mother is the exact opposite: an ithyphallic Hermes (the Egyptian Bes) or a lingam. In India this symbol is of the highest spiritual significance, and in the West Hermes is one of the most contradictory figures of Hellenistic syncretism, which was the source of extremely important spiritual developments in Western civilization. He is also the god of revelation, and in the unofficial nature philosophy of the early Middle Ages he is nothing less than the world-creating Nous itself. This mystery has perhaps found its finest expression in the words of the *Tabula smaragdina:* "omne superius sicut inferius" (as it is above, so it is below).

194   It is a psychological fact that as soon as we touch on these identifications we enter the realm of the syzygies, the paired opposites, where the One is never separated from the Other, its antithesis. It is a field of personal experience which leads directly to the experience of individuation, the attainment of the self. A vast number of symbols for this process could be mustered from the medieval literature of the West and even more

5 Obviously a daughter can idealize her mother too, but for this special circumstances are needed, whereas in a man idealization is almost the normal thing.

from the storehouses of Oriental wisdom, but in this matter words and ideas count for little. Indeed, they may become dangerous bypaths and false trails. In this still very obscure field of psychological experience, where we are in direct contact, so to speak, with the archetype, its psychic power is felt in full force. This realm is so entirely one of immediate experience that it cannot be captured by any formula, but can only be hinted at to one who already knows. He will need no explanations to understand what was the tension of opposites expressed by Apuleius in his magnificent prayer to the Queen of Heaven, when he associates "heavenly Venus" with "Proserpina, who strikest terror with midnight ululations": [6] it was the terrifying paradox of the primordial mother-image.

*

195   When, in 1938, I originally wrote this paper, I naturally did not know that twelve years later the Christian version of the mother archetype would be elevated to the rank of a dogmatic truth. The Christian "Queen of Heaven" has, obviously, shed all her Olympian qualities except for her brightness, goodness, and eternality; and even her human body, the thing most prone to gross material corruption, has put on an ethereal incorruptibility. The richly varied allegories of the Mother of God have nevertheless retained some connection with her pagan prefigurations in Isis (Io) and Semele. Not only are Isis and the Horus-child iconological exemplars, but the ascension of Semele, the originally mortal mother of Dionysus. likewise anticipates the Assumption of the Blessed Virgin. Further, this son of Semele is a dying and resurgent god and the youngest of the Olympians. Semele herself seems to have been an earth-goddess, just as the Virgin Mary is the earth from which Christ was born. This being so, the question naturally arises for the psychologist: what has become of the characteristic relation of the mother-image to the earth, darkness, the abysmal side of the bodily man with his animal passions and instinctual nature, and to "matter" in general? The declaration of the dogma comes at a time when the achievements of science and technology, combined with a rationalistic and materialistic view of the world, threaten

6 "Nocturnis ululatibus horrenda Proserpina." Cf. *Symbols of Transformation*, p. 99.

the spiritual and psychic heritage of man with instant annihilation. Humanity is arming itself, in dread and fascinated horror, for a stupendous crime. Circumstances might easily arise when the hydrogen bomb would have to be used and the unthinkably frightful deed became unavoidable in legitimate self-defence. In striking contrast to this disastrous turn of events, the Mother of God is now enthroned in heaven; indeed, her Assumption has actually been interprcted as a deliberate counterstroke to the materialistic doctrinairism that provoked the chthonic powers into revolt. Just as Christ's appearance in his own day created a real devil and adversary of God out of what was originally a son of God dwelling in heaven, so now, conversely, a heavenly figure has split off from her original chthonic realm and taken up a counter-position to the titanic forces of the earth and the underworld that have been unleashed. In the same way that the Mother of God was divested of all the essential qualities of materiality, matter became completely de-souled, and this at a time when physics is pushing forward to insights which, if they do not exactly "de-materialize" matter, at least endue it with properties of its own and make its relation to the psyche a problem that can no longer be shelved. For just as the tremendous advancement of science led at first to a premature dethronement of mind and to an equally ill-considered deification of matter, so it is this same urge for scientific knowledge that is now attempting to bridge the huge gulf that has opened out between the two *Weltanschauungen*. The psychologist inclines to see in the dogma of the Assumption a symbol which, in a sense, anticipates this whole development. For him the relationship to the earth and to matter is one of the inalienable qualities of the mother archetype. So that when a figure that is conditioned by this archetype is represented as having been taken up into heaven, the realm of the spirit, this indicates a union of earth and heaven, or of matter and spirit. The approach of natural science will almost certainly be from the other direction: it will see in matter itself the equivalent of spirit, but this "spirit" will appear divested of all, or at any rate most, of its known qualities, just as earthly matter was stripped of its specific characteristics when it staged its entry into heaven. Nevertheless, the way will gradually be cleared for a union of the two principles.

196   Understood concretely, the Assumption is the absolute opposite of materialism. Taken in this sense, it is a counterstroke that
does nothing to diminish the tension between the opposites, but
drives it to extremes.

197   Understood symbolically, however, the Assumption of the
body is a recognition and acknowledgment of matter, which in
the last resort was identified with evil only because of an over-
whelmingly "pneumatic" tendency in man. In themselves, spirit
and matter are neutral, or rather, "utriusque capax"—that is,
capable of what man calls good or evil. Although as names they
are exceedingly relative, underlying them are very real opposites
that are part of the energic structure of the physical and of the
psychic world, and without them no existence of any kind could
be established. There is no position without its negation. In
spite or just because of their extreme opposition, neither can exist
without the other. It is exactly as formulated in classical Chinese
philosophy: *yang* (the light, warm, dry, masculine principle)
contains within it the seed of *yin* (the dark, cold, moist, feminine
principle), and vice versa. Matter therefore would contain the
seed of spirit and spirit the seed of matter. The long-known
"synchronistic" phenomena that have now been statistically
confirmed by Rhine's experiments [7] point, to all appearances,
in this direction. The "psychization" of matter puts the absolute
immateriality of spirit in question, since this would then have
to be accorded a kind of substantiality. The dogma of the Assumption, proclaimed in an age suffering from the greatest
political schism history has ever known, is a compensating
symptom that reflects the strivings of science for a uniform
world-picture. In a certain sense, both developments were anticipated by alchemy in the *hieros gamos* of opposites, but only in
symbolic form. Nevertheless, the symbol has the great advantage
of being able to unite heterogeneous or even incommensurable
factors in a *single* image. With the decline of alchemy the
symbolical unity of spirit and matter fell apart, with the result
that modern man finds himself uprooted and alienated in a
de-souled world.

198   The alchemist saw the union of opposites under the symbol
of the tree, and it is therefore not surprising that the unconscious of present-day man, who no longer feels at home in his

7 Cf. my "Synchronicity: An Acausal Connecting Principle."

world and can base his existence neither on the past that is no more nor on the future that is yet to be, should hark back to the symbol of the cosmic tree rooted in this world and growing up to heaven—the tree that is also man. In the history of symbols this tree is described as the way of life itself, a growing into that which eternally is and does not change; which springs from the union of opposites and, by its eternal presence, also makes that union possible. It seems as if it were only through an experience of symbolic reality that man, vainly seeking his own "existence" and making a philosophy out of it, can find his way back to a world in which he is no longer a stranger.

II

CONCERNING REBIRTH

This paper represents the substance of a lecture which I delivered on the spur of the moment at the Eranos meeting in 1939. In putting it into written form I have made use of the stenographic notes which were taken at the meeting. Certain portions had to be omitted, chiefly because the requirements of a printed text are different from those of the spoken word. However, so far as possible, I have carried out my original intention of summing up the content of my lecture on the theme of rebirth, and have also endeavoured to reproduce my analysis of the Eighteenth Sura of the Koran as an example of a rebirth mystery. I have added some references to source material, which the reader may welcome. My summary does not purport to be more than a survey of a field of knowledge which can only be treated very superficially in the framework of a lecture.—C. G. J.

[First published as a lecture, "Die verschiedenen Aspekte der Wiedergeburt," in *Eranos-Jahrbuch 1939* (Zurich, 1940). Revised and expanded as "Über Wiedergeburt," *Gestaltungen des Unbewussten* (Zurich, 1950), from which the present translation is made.—EDITORS.]

1. FORMS OF REBIRTH

199　　The concept of rebirth is not always used in the same sense. Since this concept has various aspects, it may be useful to review its different meanings. The five different forms which I am going to enumerate could probably be added to if one were to go into greater detail, but I venture to think that my definitions cover at least the cardinal meanings. In the first part of my exposition, I give a brief summary of the different forms of rebirth, while the second part presents its various psychological aspects. In the third part, I give an example of a rebirth mystery from the Koran.

200　　1. *Metempsychosis.* The first of the five aspects of rebirth to which I should like to draw attention is that of metempsychosis, or transmigration of souls. According to this view, one's life is prolonged in time by passing through different bodily existences; or, from another point of view, it is a life-sequence interrupted by different reincarnations. Even in Buddhism, where this doctrine is of particular importance—the Buddha himself experienced a very long sequence of such rebirths—it is by no means certain whether continuity of personality is guaranteed or not: there may be only a continuity of *karma*. The Buddha's disciples put this question to him during his lifetime, but he never made any definite statement as to whether there is or is not a continuity of personality.[1]

201　　2. *Reincarnation.* This concept of rebirth necessarily implies the continuity of personality. Here the human personality is regarded as continuous and accessible to memory, so that, when one is incarnated or born, one is able, at least potentially, to remember that one has lived through previous existences and that these existences were one's own, i.e., that they had the same ego-form as the present life. As a rule, reincarnation means rebirth in a human body.

---

[1] Cf. the *Samyutta-Nikaya (Book of the Kindred Sayings),* Part II: The Nidana Book, pp. 150f.

202 3. *Resurrection.* This means a re-establishment of human existence after death. A new element enters here: that of the change, transmutation, or transformation of one's being. The change may be either essential, in the sense that the resurrected being is a different one; or nonessential, in the sense that only the general conditions of existence have changed, as when one finds oneself in a different place or in a body which is differently constituted. It may be a carnal body, as in the Christian assumption that this body will be resurrected. On a higher level, the process is no longer understood in a gross material sense; it is assumed that the resurrection of the dead is the raising up of the *corpus glorificationis,* the "subtle body," in the state of incorruptibility.

203 4. *Rebirth (renovatio).* The fourth form concerns rebirth in the strict sense; that is to say, rebirth within the span of individual life. The English word *rebirth* is the exact equivalent of the German *Wiedergeburt,* but the French language seems to lack a term having the peculiar meaning of "rebirth." This word has a special flavour; its whole atmosphere suggests the idea of *renovatio,* renewal, or even of improvement brought about by magical means. Rebirth may be a renewal without any change of being, inasmuch as the personality which is renewed is not changed in its essential nature, but only its functions, or parts of the personality, are subjected to healing, strengthening, or improvement. Thus even bodily ills may be healed through rebirth ceremonies.

204 Another aspect of this fourth form is essential transformation, i.e., total rebirth of the individual. Here the renewal implies a change of his essential nature, and may be called a transmutation. As examples we may mention the transformation of a mortal into an immortal being, of a corporeal into a spiritual being, and of a human into a divine being. Well-known prototypes of this change are the transfiguration and ascension of Christ, and the assumption of the Mother of God into heaven after her death, together with her body. Similar conceptions are to be found in Part II of Goethe's *Faust;* for instance, the transformation of Faust into the boy and then into Doctor Marianus.

205 5. *Participation in the process of transformation.* The fifth and last form is indirect rebirth. Here the transformation is

48

brought about not directly, by passing through death and rebirth oneself, but indirectly, by participating in a process of transformation which is conceived of as taking place outside the individual. In other words, one has to witness, or take part in, some rite of transformation. This rite may be a ceremony such as the Mass, where there is a transformation of substances. Through his presence at the rite the individual participates in divine grace. Similar transformations of the Deity are to be found in the pagan mysteries; there too the initiate sharing the experience is vouchsafed the gift of grace, as we know from the Eleusinian mysteries. A case in point is the confession of the initiate in the Eleusinian mysteries, who praises the grace conferred through the certainty of immortality.[2]

2 Cf. the Homeric Hymn to Demeter, verses 480–82: "Blessed is he among men who has seen these mysteries; but he who is uninitiate and has no part in them, never has lot of like good things once he is dead, down in the darkness and gloom." (Trans. by Evelyn-White, *Hesiod, the Homeric Hymns and Homerica*, p. 323.) And in an Eleusinian epitaph we read:
> "Truly the blessed gods have proclaimed a most beautiful secret:
> Death comes not as a curse, but as a blessing to men."

2. THE PSYCHOLOGY OF REBIRTH

206   Rebirth is not a process that we can in any way observe. We can neither measure nor weigh nor photograph it. It is entirely beyond sense perception. We have to do here with a purely *psychic* reality, which is transmitted to us only indirectly through personal statements. One speaks of rebirth; one professes rebirth; one is filled with rebirth. This we accept as sufficiently real. We are not concerned here with the question: is rebirth a tangible process of some sort? We have to be content with its psychic reality. I hasten to add that I am not alluding to the vulgar notion that anything "psychic" is either nothing at all or at best even more tenuous than a gas. Quite the contrary; I am of the opinion that the psyche is the most tremendous fact of human life. Indeed, it is the mother of all human facts; of civilization and of its destroyer, war. All this is at first psychic and invisible. So long as it is "merely" psychic it cannot be experienced by the senses, but is nonetheless indisputably real. The mere fact that people talk about rebirth, and that there is such a concept at all, means that a store of psychic experiences designated by that term must actually exist. What these experiences are like we can only infer from the statements that have been made about them. So, if we want to find out what rebirth really is, we must turn to history in order to ascertain what "rebirth" has been understood to mean.

207   Rebirth is an affirmation that must be counted among the primordial affirmations of mankind. These primordial affirmations are based on what I call archetypes. In view of the fact that all affirmations relating to the sphere of the suprasensual are, in the last analysis, invariably determined by archetypes, it is not surprising that a concurrence of affirmations concerning rebirth can be found among the most widely differing peoples. There must be psychic events underlying these affirmations which it is the business of psychology to discuss—without entering into all the metaphysical and philosophical assumptions regarding their

significance. In order to obtain a general view of their phenomenology, it is necessary to sketch the whole field of transformation experiences in sharper outline. Two main groups of experience may be distinguished: that of the transcendence of life, and that of one's own transformation.

I. EXPERIENCE OF THE TRANSCENDENCE OF LIFE

208   a. *Experiences induced by ritual.*   By the "transcendence of life" I mean those aforementioned experiences of the initiate who takes part in a sacred rite which reveals to him the perpetual continuation of life through transformation and renewal. In these mystery-dramas the transcendence of life, as distinct from its momentary concrete manifestations, is usually represented by the fateful transformations—death and rebirth—of a god or a godlike hero. The initiate may either be a mere witness of the divine drama or take part in it or be moved by it, or he may see himself identified through the ritual action with the god. In this case, what really matters is that an objective substance or form of life is ritually transformed through some process going on independently, while the initiate is influenced, impressed, "consecrated," or granted "divine grace" on the mere ground of his presence or participation. The transformation process takes place not within him but outside him, although he may become involved in it. The initiate who ritually enacts the slaying, dismemberment, and scattering of Osiris, and afterwards his resurrection in the green wheat, experiences in this way the permanence and continuity of life, which outlasts all changes of form and, phoenix-like, continually rises anew from its own ashes. This participation in the ritual event gives rise, among other effects, to that hope of immortality which is characteristic of the Eleusinian mysteries.[1]

209   A living example of the mystery drama representing the permanence as well as the transformation of life is the Mass. If we observe the congregation during this sacred rite we note all degrees of participation, from mere indifferent attendance to the profoundest emotion. The groups of men standing about

1 [Cf. infra, "The Psychology of the Kore," and Kerényi's companion essays in *Essays on a Science of Mythology.*—EDITORS.]

near the exit, who are obviously engaged in every sort of worldly conversation, crossing themselves and genuflecting in a purely mechanical way—even they, despite their inattention, participate in the sacral action by their mere presence in this place where grace abounds. The Mass is an extramundane and extratemporal act in which Christ is sacrificed and then resurrected in the transformed substances; and this rite of his sacrificial death is not a repetition of the historical event but the original, unique, and eternal act. The experience of the Mass is therefore a participation in the transcendence of life, which overcomes all bounds of space and time. It is a moment of eternity in time.[2]

210   b. *Immediate Experiences.* All that the mystery drama represents and brings about in the spectator may also occur in the form of a spontaneous, ecstatic, or visionary experience, without any ritual. Nietzsche's Noontide Vision is a classic example of this kind.[3] Nietzsche, as we know, substitutes for the Christian mystery the myth of Dionysus-Zagreus, who was dismembered and came to life again. His experience has the character of a Dionysian nature myth: the Deity appears in the garb of Nature, as classical antiquity saw it,[4] and the moment of eternity is the noonday hour, sacred to Pan: "Hath time flown away? Do I not fall? Have I not fallen—hark!—into the well of eternity?" Even the "golden ring," the "ring of return," appears to him as a promise of resurrection and life.[5] It is just as if Nietzsche had been present at a performance of the mysteries.

211   Many mystic experiences have a similar character: they represent an action in which the spectator becomes involved though his nature is not necessarily changed. In the same way, the most beautiful and impressive dreams often have no lasting or transformative effect on the dreamer. He may be impressed by them, but he does not necessarily see any problem in them. The event then naturally remains "outside," like a ritual action performed by others. These more aesthetic forms of experience must be carefully distinguished from those which indubitably involve a change of one's nature.

---

[2] Cf. my "Transformation Symbolism in the Mass."
[3] *Thus Spake Zarathustra*, trans. by Common, pp. 315ff.
[4] Ibid.: "An old, bent and gnarled tree, hung with grapes."
[5] Horneffer, *Nietzsches Lehre von der ewigen Wiederkehr.*

II. SUBJECTIVE TRANSFORMATION

212   Transformations of personality are by no means rare occur-
rences. Indeed, they play a considerable role in psychopathology,
although they are rather different from the mystical experiences
just discussed, which are not easily accessible to psychological
investigation. However, the phenomena we are now about to
examine belong to a sphere quite familiar to psychology.

213   a. *Diminution of personality.*   An example of the alteration
of personality in the sense of diminution is furnished by what is
known in primitive psychology as "loss of soul." The peculiar
condition covered by this term is accounted for in the mind of
the primitive by the supposition that a soul has gone off, just
like a dog that runs away from his master overnight. It is then
the task of the medicine-man to fetch the fugitive back. Often
the loss occurs suddenly and manifests itself in a general ma-
laise. The phenomenon is closely connected with the nature of
primitive consciousness, which lacks the firm coherence of our
own. We have control of our will power, but the primitive has
not. Complicated exercises are needed if he is to pull himself
together for any activity that is conscious and intentional and
not just emotional and instinctive. Our consciousness is safer
and more dependable in this respect; but occasionally something
similar can happen to civilized man, only he does not describe
it as "loss of soul" but as an "abaissement du niveau mental,"
Janet's apt term for this phenomenon.[6] It is a slackening of the
tensity of consciousness, which might be compared to a low
barometric reading, presaging bad weather. The tonus has given
way, and this is felt subjectively as listlessness, moroseness, and
depression. One no longer has any wish or courage to face the
tasks of the day. One feels like lead, because no part of one's
body seems willing to move, and this is due to the fact that one
no longer has any disposable energy.[7] This well-known phenomenon corresponds to the primitive's loss of soul. The listlessness and paralysis of will can go so far that the whole
personality falls apart, so to speak, and consciousness loses its

6 *Les Névroses,* p. 358.

7 The *gana* phenomena described by Count Keyserling (*South-American Meditations,* pp. 161ff.) come into this category.

unity; the individual parts of the personality make themselves independent and thus escape from the control of the conscious mind, as in the case of anaesthetic areas or systematic amnesias. The latter are well known as hysterical "loss of function" phenomena. This medical term is analogous to the primitive loss of soul.

214 *Abaissement du niveau mental* can be the result of physical and mental fatigue, bodily illness, violent emotions, and shock, of which the last has a particularly deleterious effect on one's self-assurance. The *abaissement* always has a restrictive influence on the personality as a whole. It reduces one's self-confidence and the spirit of enterprise, and, as a result of increasing egocentricity, narrows the mental horizon. In the end it may lead to the development of an essentially negative personality, which means that a falsification of the original personality has supervened.

215 b. *Enlargement of personality.* The personality is seldom, in the beginning, what it will be later on. For this reason the possibility of enlarging it exists, at least during the first half of life. The enlargement may be effected through an accretion from without, by new vital contents finding their way into the personality from outside and being assimilated. In this way a considerable increase of personality may be experienced. We therefore tend to assume that this increase comes *only* from without, thus justifying the prejudice that one becomes a personality by stuffing into oneself as much as possible from outside. But the more assiduously we follow this recipe, and the more stubbornly we believe that all increase has to come from without, the greater becomes our inner poverty. Therefore, if some great idea takes hold of us from outside, we must understand that it takes hold of us only because something in us responds to it and goes out to meet it. Richness of mind consists in mental receptivity, not in the accumulation of possessions. What comes to us from outside, and, for that matter, everything that rises up from within, can only be made our own if we are capable of an inner amplitude equal to that of the incoming content. Real increase of personality means consciousness of an enlargement that flows from inner sources. Without psychic depth we can never be adequately related to the magnitude of our object. It has therefore been said quite truly that a man grows with the

greatness of his task. But he must have within himself the capacity to grow; otherwise even the most difficult task is of no benefit to him. More likely he will be shattered by it.

216   A classic example of enlargement is Nietzsche's encounter with Zarathustra, which made of the critic and aphorist a tragic poet and prophet. Another example is St. Paul, who, on his way to Damascus, was suddenly confronted by Christ. True though it may be that this Christ of St. Paul's would hardly have been possible without the historical Jesus, the apparition of Christ came to St. Paul not from the historical Jesus but from the depths of his own unconscious.

217   When a summit of life is reached, when the bud unfolds and from the lesser the greater emerges, then, as Nietzsche says, "One becomes Two," and the greater figure, which one always was but which remained invisible, appears to the lesser personality with the force of a revelation. He who is truly and hopelessly little will always drag the revelation of the greater down to the level of his littleness, and will never understand that the day of judgment for his littleness has dawned. But the man who is inwardly great will know that the long expected friend of his soul, the immortal one, has now really come, "to lead captivity captive"; [8] that is, to seize hold of him by whom this immortal had always been confined and held prisoner, and to make his life flow into that greater life—a moment of deadliest peril! Nietzsche's prophetic vision of the Tightrope Walker [9] reveals the awful danger that lies in having a "tightrope-walking" attitude towards an event to which St. Paul gave the most exalted name he could find.

218   Christ himself is the perfect symbol of the hidden immortal within the mortal man.[10] Ordinarily this problem is symbolized by a dual motif such as the Dioscuri, one of whom is mortal and the other immortal. An Indian parallel is the parable of the two friends:

> Behold, upon the selfsame tree,
> Two birds, fast-bound companions, sit.

8 Ephesians 4 : 8.

9 "Thy soul will be dead even sooner than thy body." *Thus Spake Zarathustra,* p. 74.

10 Cf. "A Psychological Approach to the Dogma of the Trinity," pars. 226ff.

> This one enjoys the ripened fruit,
> The other looks, but does not eat.
>
> On such a tree my spirit crouched,
> Deluded by its powerlessness,
> Till seeing with joy how great its Lord,
> It found from sorrow swift release. . . .[11]

219   Another notable parallel is the Islamic legend of the meeting of Moses and Khidr,[12] to which I shall return later on. Naturally the transformation of personality in this enlarging sense does not occur only in the form of such highly significant experiences. There is no lack of more trivial instances, a list of which could easily be compiled from the clinical history of neurotic patients. Indeed, any case where the recognition of a greater personality seems to burst an iron ring round the heart must be included in this category.[13]

220   c. *Change of internal structure.* We now come to changes of personality which imply neither enlargement nor diminution but a structural alteration. One of the most important forms is the phenomenon of possession: some content, an idea or a part of the personality, obtains mastery of the individual for one reason or another. The contents which thus take possession appear as peculiar convictions, idiosyncrasies, stubborn plans, and so forth. As a rule, they are not open to correction. One has to be an especially good friend of the possessed person and willing to put up with almost anything if one is to attempt to deal with such a condition. I am not prepared to lay down any hard and fast line of demarcation between possession and paranoia. Possession can be formulated as identity of the ego-personality with a complex.[14]

221   A common instance of this is identity with the persona, which is the individual's system of adaptation to, or the manner he assumes in dealing with, the world. Every calling or profes-

---

[11] Shvetashvatara Upanishad 4, 6ff. (Trans. based on Hume, *The Thirteen Principal Upanishads*, pp. 403ff.).

[12] Koran, 18th Sura.

[13] I have discussed one such case of a widening of the personality in my inaugural dissertation, "On the Psychology and Pathology of So-called Occult Phenomena."

[14] For the Church's view of possession see de Tonquédec, *Les Maladies nerveuses ou mentales et les manifestations diaboliques;* also "A Psychological Approach to the Dogma of the Trinity," p. 163, n. 15.

sion, for example, has its own characteristic persona. It is easy to study these things nowadays, when the photographs of public personalities so frequently appear in the press. A certain kind of behaviour is forced on them by the world, and professional people endeavour to come up to these expectations. Only, the danger is that they become identical with their personas—the professor with his text-book, the tenor with his voice. Then the damage is done; henceforth he lives exclusively against the background of his own biography. For by that time it is written: ". . . then he went to such and such a place and said this or that," etc. The garment of Deianeira has grown fast to his skin, and a desperate decision like that of Heracles is needed if he is to tear this Nessus shirt from his body and step into the consuming fire of the flame of immortality, in order to transform himself into what he really is. One could say, with a little exaggeration, that the persona is that which in reality one is not, but which oneself as well as others think one is.[15] In any case the temptation to be what one seems to be is great, because the persona is usually rewarded in cash.

222   There are still other factors which may take possession of the individual, one of the most important being the so-called "inferior function." This is not the place to enter into a detailed discussion of this problem;[16] I should only like to point out that the inferior function is practically identical with the dark side of the human personality. The darkness which clings to every personality is the door into the unconscious and the gateway of dreams, from which those two twilight figures, the shadow and the anima, step into our nightly visions or, remaining invisible, take possession of our ego-consciousness. A man who is possessed by his shadow is always standing in his own light and falling into his own traps. Whenever possible, he prefers to make an unfavourable impression on others. In the long run luck is always against him, because he is living below his own level and at best only attains what does not suit him. And if there is no doorstep for him to stumble over, he manufactures one for himself and then fondly believes he has done something useful.

15 In this connection, Schopenhauer's "The Wisdom of Life: Aphorisms" (*Essays from the Parerga and Paralipomena*) could be read with profit.
16 This important problem is discussed in detail in Ch. II of *Psychological Types*.

223   Possession caused by the anima or animus presents a different picture. Above all, this transformation of personality gives prominence to those traits which are characteristic of the opposite sex; in man the feminine traits, and in woman the masculine. In the state of possession both figures lose their charm and their values; they retain them only when they are turned away from the world, in the introverted state, when they serve as bridges to the unconscious. Turned towards the world, the anima is fickle, capricious, moody, uncontrolled and emotional, sometimes gifted with daemonic intuitions, ruthless, malicious, untruthful, bitchy, double-faced, and mystical.[17] The animus is obstinate, harping on principles, laying down the law, dogmatic, world-reforming, theoretic, word-mongering, argumentative, and domineering.[18] Both alike have bad taste: the anima surrounds herself with inferior people, and the animus lets himself be taken in by second-rate thinking.

224   Another form of structural change concerns certain unusual observations about which I speak only with the utmost reserve. I refer to states of possession in which the possession is caused by something that could perhaps most fitly be described as an "ancestral soul," by which I mean the soul of some definite forebear. For all practical purposes, such cases may be regarded as striking instances of identification with deceased persons. (Naturally, the phenomena of identity only occur after the "ancestor's" death.) My attention was first drawn to such possibilities by Léon Daudet's confused but ingenious book *L'Hérédo*. Daudet supposes that, in the structure of the personality, there are ancestral elements which under certain conditions may suddenly come to the fore. The individual is then precipitately thrust into an ancestral role. Now we know that ancestral roles play a very important part in primitive psychology. Not only are ancestral spirits supposed to be reincarnated in children, but an attempt is made to implant them into

17 Cf. the apt description of the anima in Aldrovandus, *Dendrologiae libri duo* (1668, p. 211): "She appeared both very soft and very hard at the same time, and while for some two thousand years she had made a show of inconstant looks like a Proteus, she bedevilled the love of Lucius Agatho Priscus, then a citizen of Bologna, with anxious cares and sorrows, which assuredly were conjured up from chaos, or from what Plato calls Agathonian confusion." There is a similar description in Fierz-David, *The Dream of Poliphilo*, pp. 189ff.
18 Cf. Emma Jung, "On the Nature of the Animus."

the child by naming him after an ancestor. So, too, primitives try to change themselves back into their ancestors by means of certain rites. I would mention especially the Australian conception of the *alcheringamijina*,[19] ancestral souls, half man and half animal, whose reactivation through religious rites is of the greatest functional significance for the life of the tribe. Ideas of this sort, dating back to the Stone Age, were widely diffused, as may be seen from numerous other traces that can be found elsewhere. It is therefore not improbable that these primordial forms of experience may recur even today as cases of identification with ancestral souls, and I believe I have seen such cases.

225   d. *Identification with a group.*   We shall now discuss another form of transformation experience which I would call identification with a group. More accurately speaking, it is the identification of an individual with a number of people who, as a group, have a collective experience of transformation. This special psychological situation must not be confused with participation in a transformation rite, which, though performed before an audience, does not in any way depend upon group identity or necessarily give rise to it. To experience transformation in a group and to experience it in oneself are two totally different things. If any considerable group of persons are united and identified with one another by a particular frame of mind, the resultant transformation experience bears only a very remote resemblance to the experience of individual transformation. A group experience takes place on a lower level of consciousness than the experience of an individual. This is due to the fact that, when many people gather together to share one common emotion, the total psyche emerging from the group is below the level of the individual psyche. If it is a very large group, the collective psyche will be more like the psyche of an animal, which is the reason why the ethical attitude of large organizations is always doubtful. The psychology of a large crowd inevitably sinks to the level of mob psychology.[20] If, therefore, I have a so-called collective experience as a member of a group, it takes place on a lower level of consciousness than if I had the experience by myself alone. That is why this group experience is very much more frequent than an individual experience of transformation. It is also much easier to achieve,

19 Cf. Lévy-Bruhl, *La Mythologie primitive.*   20 Le Bon, *The Crowd.*

because the presence of so many people together exerts great suggestive force. The individual in a crowd easily becomes the victim of his own suggestibility. It is only necessary for something to happen, for instance a proposal backed by the whole crowd, and we too are all for it, even if the proposal is immoral. In the crowd one feels no responsibility, but also no fear.

226   Thus identification with the group is a simple and easy path to follow, but the group experience goes no deeper than the level of one's own mind in that state. It does work a change in you, but the change does not last. On the contrary, you must have continual recourse to mass intoxication in order to consolidate the experience and your belief in it. But as soon as you are removed from the crowd, you are a different person again and unable to reproduce the previous state of mind. The mass is swayed by *participation mystique,* which is nothing other than an unconscious identity. Supposing, for example, you go to the theatre: glance meets glance, everybody observes everybody else, so that all those who are present are caught up in an invisible web of mutual unconscious relationship. If this condition increases, one literally feels borne along by the universal wave of identity with others. It may be a pleasant feeling—one sheep among ten thousand! Again, if I feel that this crowd is a great and wonderful unity, I am a hero, exalted along with the group. When I am myself again, I discover that I am Mr. So-and-So, and that I live in such and such a street, on the third floor. I also find that the whole affair was really most delightful, and I hope it will take place again tomorrow so that I may once more feel myself to be a whole nation, which is much better than being just plain Mr. X. Since this is such an easy and convenient way of raising one's personality to a more exalted rank, mankind has always formed groups which made collective experiences of transformation—often of an ecstatic nature—possible. The regressive identification with lower and more primitive states of consciousness is invariably accompanied by a heightened sense of life; hence the quickening effect of regressive identifications with half-animal ancestors [21] in the Stone Age.

227   The inevitable psychological regression within the group is

21 The *alcheringamijina.* Cf. the rites of Australian tribes, in Spencer and Gillen, *The Northern Tribes of Central Australia;* also Lévy-Bruhl, *La Mythologie primitive.*

partially counteracted by ritual, that is to say through a cult ceremony which makes the solemn performance of sacred events the centre of group activity and prevents the crowd from relapsing into unconscious instinctuality. By engaging the individual's interest and attention, the ritual makes it possible for him to have a comparatively individual experience even within the group and so to remain more or less conscious. But if there is no relation to a centre which expresses the unconscious through its symbolism, the mass psyche inevitably becomes the hypnotic focus of fascination, drawing everyone under its spell. That is why masses are always breeding-grounds of psychic epidemics,[22] the events in Germany being a classic example of this.

228   It will be objected to this essentially negative evaluation of mass psychology that there are also positive experiences, for instance a positive enthusiasm which spurs the individual to noble deeds, or an equally positive feeling of human solidarity. Facts of this kind should not be denied. The group can give the individual a courage, a bearing, and a dignity which may easily get lost in isolation. It can awaken within him the memory of being a man among men. But that does not prevent something else from being added which he would not possess as an individual. Such unearned gifts may seem a special favour of the moment, but in the long run there is a danger of the gift becoming a loss, since human nature has a weak habit of taking gifts for granted; in times of necessity we demand them as a right instead of making the effort to obtain them ourselves. One sees this, unfortunately, only too plainly in the tendency to demand everything from the State, without reflecting that the State consists of those very individuals who make the demands. The logical development of this tendency leads to Communism, where each individual enslaves the community and the latter is represented by a dictator, the slave-owner. All primitive tribes characterized by a communistic order of society also have a chieftain over them with unlimited powers. The Communist State is nothing other than an absolute monarchy in which there are no subjects, but only serfs.

22 I would remind the reader of the catastrophic panic which broke out in New York on the occasion [1938] of a broadcast dramatization of H. G. Wells' *War of the Worlds* shortly before the second World War [see Cantril, *The Invasion from Mars* (1940)], and which was later [1949] repeated in Quito.

229   e. *Identification with a cult-hero.*   Another important identification underlying the transformation experience is that with
the god or hero who is transformed in the sacred ritual. Many
cult ceremonies are expressly intended to bring this identity
about, an obvious example being the *Metamorphosis* of Apuleius. The initiate, an ordinary human being, is elected to be
Helios; he is crowned with a crown of palms and clad in the
mystic mantle, whereupon the assembled crowd pays homage to
him. The suggestion of the crowd brings about his identity with
the god. The participation of the community can also take place
in the following way: there is no apotheosis of the initiate, but
the sacred action is recited, and then, in the course of long
periods of time, psychic changes gradually occur in the individual participants. The Osiris cult offers an excellent example of
this. At first only Pharaoh participated in the transformation of
the god, since he alone "had an Osiris"; but later the nobles
of the Empire acquired an Osiris too, and finally this development culminated in the Christian idea that everyone has an
immortal soul and shares directly in the Godhead. In Christianity the development was carried still further when the outer
God or Christ gradually became the inner Christ of the individual believer, remaining one and the same though dwelling in
many. This truth had already been anticipated by the psychology of totemism: many exemplars of the totem animal are
killed and consumed during the totem meals, and yet it is only
the One who is being eaten, just as there is only one Christ-child
and one Santa Claus.

230   In the mysteries, the individual undergoes an indirect transformation through his participation in the fate of the god. The
transformation experience is also an indirect one in the Christian Church, inasmuch as it is brought about by participation in
something acted or recited. Here the first form, the *dromenon,*
is characteristic of the richly developed ritual of the Catholic
Church; the second form, the recitation, the "Word" or "gospel," is practised in the "preaching of the Word" in Protestant-
ism.

231   f. *Magical procedures.*   A further form of transformation is
achieved through a rite used directly for this purpose. Instead
of the transformation experience coming to one through participation in the rite, the rite is used for the express purpose of

effecting the transformation. It thus becomes a sort of technique to which one submits oneself. For instance, a man is ill and consequently needs to be "renewed." The renewal must "happen" to him from outside, and to bring this about, he is pulled through a hole in the wall at the head of his sick-bed, and now he is reborn; or he is given another name and thereby another soul, and then the demons no longer recognize him; or he has to pass through a symbolical death; or, grotesquely enough, he is pulled through a leathern cow, which devours him, so to speak, in front and then expels him behind; or he undergoes an ablution or baptismal bath and miraculously changes into a semi-divine being with a new character and an altered metaphysical destiny.

232   g. *Technical transformation.*   Besides the use of the rite in the magical sense, there are still other special techniques in which, in addition to the grace inherent in the rite, the personal endeavour of the initiate is needed in order to achieve the intended purpose. It is a transformation experience induced by technical means. The exercises known in the East as yoga and in the West as *exercitia spiritualia* come into this category. These exercises represent special techniques prescribed in advance and intended to achieve a definite psychic effect, or at least to promote it. This is true both of Eastern yoga and of the methods practised in the West.[23] They are, therefore, technical procedures in the fullest sense of the word; elaborations of the originally natural processes of transformation. The natural or spontaneous transformations that occurred earlier, before there were any historical examples to follow, were thus replaced by techniques designed to induce the transformation by imitating this same sequence of events. I will try to give an idea of the way such techniques may have originated by relating a fairy story:

233   There was once a queer old man who lived in a cave, where he had sought refuge from the noise of the villages. He was reputed to be a sorcerer, and therefore he had disciples who hoped to learn the art of sorcery from him. But he himself was not thinking of any such thing. He was only seeking to know what it was that he did not know, but which, he felt certain, was always happening. After meditating for a very long time on

23 Cf. "The Psychology of Eastern Meditation."

that which is beyond meditation, he saw no other way of escape from his predicament than to take a piece of red chalk and draw all kinds of diagrams on the walls of his cave, in order to find out what that which he did not know might look like. After many attempts he hit on the circle. "That's right," he felt, "and now for a quadrangle inside it!"—which made it better still. His disciples were curious; but all they could make out was that the old man was up to something, and they would have given anything to know what he was doing. But when they asked him: "What are you doing there?" he made no reply. Then they discovered the diagrams on the wall and said: "That's it!"—and they all imitated the diagrams. But in so doing they turned the whole process upside down, without noticing it: they anticipated the result in the hope of making the process repeat itself which had led to that result. This is how it happened then and how it still happens today.

234   h. *Natural transformation (individuation)*. As I have pointed out, in addition to the technical processes of transformation there are also natural transformations. All ideas of rebirth are founded on this fact. Nature herself demands a death and a rebirth. As the alchemist Democritus says: "Nature rejoices in nature, nature subdues nature, nature rules over nature." There are natural transformation processes which simply happen to us, whether we like it or not, and whether we know it or not. These processes develop considerable psychic effects, which would be sufficient in themselves to make any thoughtful person ask himself what really happened to him. Like the old man in our fairytale, he, too, will draw mandalas and seek shelter in their protective circle; in the perplexity and anguish of his self-chosen prison, which he had deemed a refuge, he is transformed into a being akin to the gods. Mandalas are birth-places, vessels of birth in the most literal sense, lotus-flowers in which a Buddha comes to life. Sitting in the lotus-seat, the yogi sees himself transfigured into an immortal.

235   Natural transformation processes announce themselves mainly in dreams. Elsewhere [24] I have presented a series of dream-symbols of the process of individuation. They were dreams which without exception exhibited rebirth symbolism. In this particular case there was a long-drawn-out process of

24 Cf. *Psychology and Alchemy*, Part II.

inner transformation and rebirth into another being. This "other being" is the other person in ourselves—that larger and greater personality maturing within us, whom we have already met as the inner friend of the soul. That is why we take comfort whenever we find the friend and companion depicted in a ritual, an example being the friendship between Mithras and the sun-god. This relationship is a mystery to the scientific intellect, because the intellect is accustomed to regard these things unsympathetically. But if it made allowance for feeling, we would discover that it is the friend whom the sun-god takes with him on his chariot, as shown in the monuments. It is the representation of a friendship between two men which is simply the outer reflection of an inner fact: it reveals our relationship to that inner friend of the soul into whom Nature herself would like to change us—that other person who we also are and yet can never attain to completely. We are that pair of Dioscuri, one of whom is mortal and the other immortal, and who, though always together, can never be made completely one. The transformation processes strive to approximate them to one another, but our consciousness is aware of resistances, because the other person seems strange and uncanny, and because we cannot get accustomed to the idea that we are not absolute master in our own house. We should prefer to be always "I" and nothing else. But we are confronted with that inner friend or foe, and whether he is our friend or our foe depends on ourselves.

236   You need not be insane to hear his voice. On the contrary, it is the simplest and most natural thing imaginable. For instance, you can ask yourself a question to which "he" gives answer. The discussion is then carried on as in any other conversation. You can describe it as mere "associating" or "talking to oneself," or as a "meditation" in the sense used by the old alchemists, who referred to their interlocutor as *aliquem alium internum,* 'a certain other one, within.' [25] This form of colloquy with the friend of the soul was even admitted by Ignatius Loyola into the technique of his *Exercitia spiritualia,*[26] but with the limiting condition that only the person meditating is

25 Cf. Ruland, *Lexicon* (1893 edn.), p. 226.
26 Izquierdo, *Pratica di alcuni Esercitij spirituali di S. Ignatio* (Rome, 1686, p. 7): "A colloquy . . . is nothing else than to talk and communicate familiarly with Christ."

allowed to speak, whereas the inner responses are passed over as being merely human and therefore to be repudiated. This state of things has continued down to the present day. It is no longer a moral or metaphysical prejudice, but—what is much worse—an intellectual one. The "voice" is explained as nothing but "associating," pursued in a witless way and running on and on without sense or purpose, like the works of a clock that has no dial. Or we say "It is only my own thoughts!" even if, on closer inspection, it should turn out that they are thoughts which we either reject or had never consciously thought at all—as if everything psychic that is glimpsed by the ego had always formed part of it! Naturally this hybris serves the useful purpose of maintaining the supremacy of ego-consciousness, which must be safeguarded against dissolution into the unconscious. But it breaks down ignominiously if ever the unconscious should choose to let some nonsensical idea become an obsession or to produce other psychogenic symptoms, for which we would not like to accept responsibility on any account.

²37 Our attitude towards this inner voice alternates between two extremes: it is regarded either as undiluted nonsense or as the voice of God. It does not seem to occur to any one that there might be something valuable in between. The "other" may be just as one-sided in one way as the ego is in another. And yet the conflict between them may give rise to truth and meaning—but only if the ego is willing to grant the other its rightful personality. It has, of course, a personality anyway, just as have the voices of insane people; but a real colloquy becomes possible only when the ego acknowledges the existence of a partner to the discussion. This cannot be expected of everyone, because, after all, not everyone is a fit subject for *exercitia spiritualia*. Nor can it be called a colloquy if one speaks only to oneself or only addresses the other, as is the case with George Sand in her conversations with a "spiritual friend": ²⁶ᵃ for thirty pages she talks exclusively to herself while one waits in vain for the other to reply. The colloquy of the *exercitia* may be followed by that silent grace in which the modern doubter no longer believes. But what if it were the supplicated Christ himself who gave immediate answer in the words of the sinful human heart? What fearful abysses of doubt would then be opened? What madness

²⁶ᵃ ["Daily Conversations with Dr. Piffoel," in her *Intimate Journal*.—EDITORS.]

should we not then have to fear? From this one can understand
that images of the gods are better mute, and that ego-consciousness had better believe in its own supremacy rather than go on
"associating." One can also understand why that inner friend
so often seems to be our enemy, and why he is so far off and
his voice so low. For he who is near to him "is near to the fire."

238   Something of this sort may have been in the mind of the
alchemist who wrote: "Choose for your Stone him through
whom kings are honoured in their crowns, and through whom
physicians heal their sick, for he is near to the fire." [27] The alchemists projected the inner event into an outer figure, so for
them the inner friend appeared in the form of the "Stone," of
which the *Tractatus aureus* says: "Understand, ye sons of the
wise, what this exceeding precious Stone crieth out to you:
Protect me and I will protect thee. Give me what is mine that
I may help thee." [28] To this a scholiast adds: "The seeker after
truth hears both the Stone and the Philosopher speaking as if
out of one mouth." [29] The Philosopher is Hermes, and the
Stone is identical with Mercurius, the Latin Hermes.[30] From
the earliest times, Hermes was the mystagogue and psychopomp
of the alchemists, their friend and counsellor, who leads them
to the goal of their work. He is "like a teacher mediating between the stone and the disciple." [31] To others the friend appears in the shape of Christ or Khidr or a visible or invisible
guru, or some other personal guide or leader figure. In this
case the colloquy is distinctly one-sided: there is no inner dia-

27 A Pseudo-Aristotle quotation in *Rosarium philosophorum* (1550), fol. Q.
28 "Largiri vis mihi meum" is the usual reading, as in the first edition (1556) of
Ars chemica, under the title "Septem tractatus seu capitula Hermetis Trismegisti
aurei," and also in *Theatrum chemicum,* IV (1613), and Manget, *Bibliotheca
chemica,* I (1702), pp. 400ff. In the *Rosarium philosophorum* (1550), fol. E^v,
there is a different reading: "Largire mihi ius meum ut te adiuvem" (Give me my
due that I may help thee). This is one of the interpretative readings for which
the anonymous author of the *Rosarium* is responsible. Despite their arbitrariness
they have an important bearing on the interpretation of alchemy. [Cf. *Psychology
and Alchemy,* par. 139, n.17.]   29 *Biblio. chem.,* I, p. 430b.
30 Detailed documentation in *Psychology and Alchemy,* par. 84, and "The Spirit
Mercurius," pars. 278ff., 287ff.
31 "Tanquam praeceptor intermedius inter lapidem et discipulum." (*Biblio.
chem.,* I, p. 430b.) Cf. the beautiful prayer of Astrampsychos, beginning "Come to
me, Lord Hermes," and ending "I am thou and thou art I." (Reitzenstein,
Poimandres, p. 21.)

logue, but instead the response appears as the action of the other, i.e., as an outward event. The alchemists saw it in the transformation of the chemical substance. So if one of them sought transformation, he discovered it outside in matter, whose transformation cried out to him, as it were, "I am the transformation!" But some were clever enough to know, "It is my own transformation—not a personal transformation, but the transformation of what is mortal in me into what is immortal. It shakes off the mortal husk that I am and awakens to a life of its own; it mounts the sun-barge and may take me with it." [32]

239   This is a very ancient idea. In Upper Egypt, near Aswan, I once saw an ancient Egyptian tomb that had just been opened. Just behind the entrance-door was a little basket made of reeds, containing the withered body of a new-born infant, wrapped in rags. Evidently the wife of one of the workmen had hastily laid the body of her dead child in the nobleman's tomb at the last moment, hoping that, when he entered the sun-barge in order to rise anew, it might share in his salvation, because it had been buried in the holy precinct within reach of divine grace.

[32] The stone and its transformation are represented:

(1) as the resurrection of the *homo philosophicus*, the Second Adam ("Aurea hora," *Artis auriferae*, 1593, I, p. 195);

(2) as the human soul ("Book of Krates," Berthelot, *La Chimie au moyen âge*, III, p. 50);

(3) as a being below and above man: "This stone is under thee, as to obedience; above thee, as to dominion; therefore from thee, as to knowledge; about thee, as to equals" ("Rosinus ad Sarratantam," *Art. aurif.*, I, p. 310);

(4) as life: "blood is soul and soul is life and life is our Stone" ("Tractatulus Aristotelis," ibid., p. 364),

(5) as the resurrection of the dead ("Calidis liber secretorum," ibid., p. 347; also "Rachaidibi fragmentum," ibid., p. 398);

(6) as the Virgin Mary ("De arte chymica," ibid., p. 582); and

(7) as man himself: "thou art its ore . . . and it is extracted from thee . . . and it remains inseparably with thee" ("Rosinus ad Sarratantam," ibid., p. 311).

3. A TYPICAL SET OF SYMBOLS ILLUSTRATING THE PROCESS OF TRANSFORMATION

240   I have chosen as an example a figure which plays a great role in Islamic mysticism, namely Khidr, "the Verdant One." He appears in the Eighteenth Sura of the Koran, entitled "The Cave."[1] This entire Sura is taken up with a rebirth mystery. The cave is the place of rebirth, that secret cavity in which one is shut up in order to be incubated and renewed. The Koran says of it: "You might have seen the rising sun decline to the right of their cavern, and as it set, go past them on the left, while they [the Seven Sleepers] stayed in the middle." The "middle" is the centre where the jewel reposes, where the incubation or the sacrificial rite or the transformation takes place. The most beautiful development of this symbolism is to be found on Mithraic altarpieces [2] and in alchemical pictures of the transformative substance,[3] which is always shown between sun and moon. Representations of the crucifixion frequently follow the same type, and a similar symbolical arrangement is also found in the transformation or healing ceremonies of the Navahos.[4] Just such a place of the centre or of transformation is the cave in which those seven had gone to sleep, little thinking that they would experience there a prolongation of life verging on immortality. When they awoke, they had slept 309 years.

241   The legend has the following meaning: Anyone who gets into that cave, that is to say into the cave which everyone has in himself, or into the darkness that lies behind consciousness, will find himself involved in an—at first—unconscious process of transformation. By penetrating into the unconscious he makes

1 [The Dawood trans. of the Koran is quoted, sometimes with modifications. The 18th Sura is at pp. 89–98.—EDITORS.]

2 Cumont, *Textes et monuments figurés relatifs aux mystères de Mithra*, II.

3 Cf. especially the crowning vision in the dream of Zosimos: "And another [came] behind him, bringing one adorned round with signs, clad in white and comely to see, who was named the Meridian of the Sun." Cf. "The Visions of Zosimos," par. 87 (III, v bis).

4 Matthews, *The Mountain Chant*, and Stevenson, *Ceremonial of Hasjelti Dailjis.*

a connection with his unconscious contents. This may result in a momentous change of personality in the positive or negative sense. The transformation is often interpreted as a prolongation of the natural span of life or as an earnest of immortality. The former is the case with many alchemists, notably Paracelsus (in his treatise *De vita longa* [5]), and the latter is exemplified in the Eleusinian mysteries.

242   Those seven sleepers indicate by their sacred number [6] that they are gods,[7] who are transformed during sleep and thereby enjoy eternal youth. This helps us to understand at the outset that we are dealing with a mystery legend. The fate of the numinous figures recorded in it grips the hearer, because the story gives expression to parallel processes in his own unconscious which in that way are integrated with consciousness again. The repristination of the original state is tantamount to attaining once more the freshness of youth.

243   The story of the sleepers is followed by some moral observations which appear to have no connection with it. But this apparent irrelevance is deceptive. In reality, these edifying comments are just what are needed by those who cannot be reborn themselves and have to be content with moral conduct, that is to

[5] An account of the secret doctrine hinted at in this treatise may be found in my "Paracelsus as a Spiritual Phenomenon," pars. 169ff.

[6] The different versions of the legend speak sometimes of seven and sometimes of eight disciples. According to the account given in the Koran, the eighth is a dog. The 18th Sura mentions still other versions: "Some will say: 'The sleepers were three: their dog was the fourth.' Others, guessing at the unknown, will say: 'They were five; their dog was the sixth.' And yet others: 'Seven; their dog was the eighth.'" It is evident, therefore, that the dog is to be taken into account. This would seem to be an instance of that characteristic wavering between seven and eight (or three and four, as the case may be), which I have pointed out in *Psychology and Alchemy*, pars. 200ff. There the wavering between seven and eight is connected with the appearance of Mephistopheles, who, as we know, materialized out of the black poodle. In the case of three and four, the fourth is the devil or the female principle, and on a higher level the Mater Dei. (Cf. "Psychology and Religion," pars. 124ff.) We may be dealing with the same kind of ambiguity as in the numbering of the Egyptian nonad (*paut* = 'company of gods'; cf. Budge, *The Gods of the Egyptians*, I, p. 88). The Khidr legend relates to the persecution of the Christians under Decius (*c*. A.D. 250). The scene is Ephesus, where St. John lay "sleeping," but not dead. The seven sleepers woke up again during the reign of Theodosius II (408–450); thus they had slept not quite 200 years.

[7] The seven are the planetary gods of the ancients. Cf. Bousset, *Hauptprobleme der Gnosis*, pp. 23ff.

say with adherence to the law. Very often behaviour prescribed by rule is a substitute for spiritual transformation.[8] These edifying observations are then followed by the story of Moses and his servant Joshua ben Nun:

And Moses said to his servant: "I will not cease from my wanderings until I have reached the place where the two seas meet, even though I journey for eighty years."

But when they had reached the place where the two seas meet, they forgot their fish, and it took its way through a stream to the sea.

And when they had journeyed past this place, Moses said to his servant: "Bring us our breakfast, for we are weary from this journey."

But the other replied: "See what has befallen me! When we were resting there by the rock, I forgot the fish. Only Satan can have put it out of my mind, and in wondrous fashion it took its way to the sea."

Then Moses said: "That is the place we seek." And they went back the way they had come. And they found one of Our servants, whom We had endowed with Our grace and Our wisdom. Moses said to him: "Shall I follow you, that you may teach me for my guidance some of the wisdom you have learnt?"

But he answered: "You will not bear with me, for how should you bear patiently with things you cannot comprehend?"

Moses said: "If Allah wills, you shall find me patient; I shall not in anything disobey you."

He said: "If you are bent on following me, you must ask no question about anything till I myself speak to you concerning it."

The two set forth, but as soon as they embarked, Moses' companion bored a hole in the bottom of the ship.

"A strange thing you have done!" exclaimed Moses. "Is it to drown her passengers that you have bored a hole in her?"

---

[8] Obedience under the law on the one hand, and the freedom of the "children of God," the reborn, on the other, is discussed at length in the Epistles of St. Paul. He distinguishes not only between two different classes of men, who are separated by a greater or lesser development of consciousness, but also between the higher and lower man in one and the same individual. The *sarkikos* (carnal man) remains eternally under the law; the *pneumatikos* (spiritual man) alone is capable of being reborn into freedom. This is quite in keeping with what seems such an insoluble paradox: the Church demanding absolute obedience and at the same time proclaiming freedom from the law. So, too, in the Koran text, the legend appeals to the *pneumatikos* and promises rebirth to him that has ears to hear. But he who, like the *sarkikos,* has no inner ear will find satisfaction and safe guidance in blind submission to Allah's will.

"Did I not tell you," he replied, "that you would not bear with me?"

"Pardon my forgetfulness," said Moses. "Do not be angry with me on this account."

They journeyed on until they fell in with a certain youth. Moses' companion slew him, and Moses said: "You have killed an innocent man who has done no harm. Surely you have committed a wicked crime."

"Did I not tell you," he replied, "that you would not bear with me?"

Moses said: "If ever I question you again, abandon me; for then I should deserve it."

They travelled on until they came to a certain city. They asked the people for some food, but the people declined to receive them as their guests. There they found a wall on the point of falling down. The other raised it up, and Moses said: "Had you wished, you could have demanded payment for your labours."

"Now the time has arrived when we must part," said the other. "But first I will explain to you those acts of mine which you could not bear with in patience.

"Know that the ship belonged to some poor fishermen. I damaged it because in their rear was a king who was taking every ship by force.

"As for the youth, his parents both are true believers, and we feared lest he should plague them with his wickedness and unbelief. It was our wish that their Lord should grant them another in his place, a son more righteous and more filial.

"As for the wall, it belonged to two orphan boys in the city whose father was an honest man. Beneath it their treasure is buried. Your Lord decreed in His mercy that they should dig out their treasure when they grew to manhood. What I did was not done by caprice. That is the meaning of the things you could not bear with in patience."

244   This story is an amplification and elucidation of the legend of the seven sleepers and the problem of rebirth. Moses is the man who seeks, the man on the "quest." On this pilgrimage he is accompanied by his "shadow," the "servant" or "lower" man (*pneumatikos* and *sarkikos* in two individuals). Joshua is the son of Nun, which is a name for "fish," [9] suggesting that Joshua had his origin in the depths of the waters, in the darkness of the

9 Vollers, "Chidher," *Archiv für Religionswissenschaft,* XII, p. 241. All quotations from the commentaries are extracted from this article.

shadow-world. The critical place is reached "where the two seas meet," which is interpreted as the isthmus of Suez, where the Western and the Eastern seas come close together. In other words, it is that "place of the middle" which we have already met in the symbolic preamble, but whose significance was not recognized at first by the man and his shadow. They had "forgotten their fish," the humble source of nourishment. The fish refers to Nun, the father of the shadow, of the carnal man, who comes from the dark world of the Creator. For the fish came alive again and leapt out of the basket in order to find its way back to its homeland, the sea. In other words, the animal ancestor and creator of life separates himself from the conscious man, an event which amounts to loss of the instinctive psyche. This process is a symptom of dissociation well known in the psychopathology of the neuroses; it is always connected with one-sidedness of the conscious attitude. In view of the fact, however, that neurotic phenomena are nothing but exaggerations of normal processes, it is not to be wondered at that very similar phenomena can also be found within the scope of the normal. It is a question of that well-known "loss of soul" among primitives, as described above in the section on diminution of the personality; in scientific language, an *abaissement du niveau mental*.

245 Moses and his servant soon notice what has happened. Moses had sat down, "worn out" and hungry. Evidently he had a feeling of insufficiency, for which a physiological explanation is given. Fatigue is one of the most regular symptoms of loss of energy or libido. The entire process represents something very typical, namely the *failure to recognize a moment of crucial importance,* a motif which we encounter in a great variety of mythical forms. Moses realizes that he has unconsciously found the source of life and then lost it again, which we might well regard as a remarkable intuition. The fish they had intended to eat is a content of the unconscious, by which the connection with the origin is re-established. He is the reborn one, who has awakened to new life. This came to pass, as the commentaries say, through the contact with the water of life: by slipping back into the sea, the fish once more becomes a content of the unconscious, and its offspring are distinguished by having only one eye and half a head.[10]

10 Ibid., p. 253.

246   The alchemists, too, speak of a strange fish in the sea, the "round fish lacking bones and skin," [11] which symbolizes the "round element," the germ of the "animate stone," of the *filius philosophorum*. The water of life has its parallel in the *aqua permanens* of alchemy. This water is extolled as "vivifying," besides which it has the property of dissolving all solids and coagulating all liquids. The Koran commentaries state that, on the spot where the fish disappeared, the sea was turned to solid ground, whereon the tracks of the fish could still be seen.[12] On the island thus formed Khidr was sitting, in the place of the middle. A mystical interpretation says that he was sitting "on a throne consisting of light, between the upper and the lower sea," [13] again in the middle position. The appearance of Khidr seems to be mysteriously connected with the disappearance of the fish. It looks almost as if he himself had been the fish. This conjecture is supported by the fact that the commentaries relegate the source of life to the "place of darkness." [14] The depths of the sea are dark (*mare tenebrositatis*). The darkness has its parallel in the alchemical *nigredo,* which occurs after the *coniunctio,* when the female takes the male into herself.[15] From the *nigredo* issues the Stone, the symbol of the immortal self; moreover, its first appearance is likened to "fish eyes." [16]

11 Cf. *Aion,* pars. 195ff.   12 Vollers, p. 244.

13 Ibid., p. 260.   14 Ibid., p. 258.

15 Cf. the myth in the "Visio Arislei," especially the version in the *Rosarium philosophorum (Art. aurif.,* II, p. 246), likewise the drowning of the sun in the Mercurial Fountain and the green lion who devours the sun (*Art. aurif.,* II, pp. 315, 366). Cf. "The Psychology of the Transference," pars. 467ff.

16 The white stone appears on the edge of the vessel, "like Oriental gems, like fish's eyes." Cf. Joannes Isaacus Hollandus, *Opera mineralia* (1600), p. 370. Also Lagneus, "Harmonica chemica." *Theatrum chemicum,* IV (1613), p. 870. The eyes appear at the end of the *nigredo* and with the beginning of the *albedo.* Another simile of the same sort is the *scintillae* that appear in the dark substance. This idea is traced back to Zacharias 4 : 10 (DV): "And they shall rejoice and see the tin plummet in the hand of Zorobabel. These are the seven eyes of the Lord that run to and fro through the whole earth." (Cf. Eirenaeus Orandus, in the introduction to Nicholas Flamel's *Exposition of the Hieroglyphicall Figures,* 1624, fol. A 5.) They are the seven eyes of God on the corner-stone of the new temple (Zach. 3 : 9). The number seven suggests the seven stars, the planetary gods, who were depicted by the alchemists in a cave under the earth (Mylius, *Philosophia reformata,* 1622, p. 167). They are the "sleepers enchained in Hades" (Berthelot, *Collection des anciens alchimistes grecs,* IV, xx, 8). This is an allusion to the legend of the seven sleepers.

247   Khidr may well be a symbol of the self. His qualities signalize him as such: he is said to have been born in a cave, i.e., in darkness. He is the "Long-lived One," who continually renews himself, like Elijah. Like Osiris, he is dismembered at the end of time, by Antichrist, but is able to restore himself to life. He is analogous to the Second Adam, with whom the reanimated fish is identified; [17] he is a counsellor, a Paraclete, "Brother Khidr." Anyway Moses accepts him as a higher consciousness and looks up to him for instruction. Then follow those incomprehensible deeds which show how ego-consciousness reacts to the superior guidance of the self through the twists and turns of fate. To the initiate who is capable of transformation it is a comforting tale; to the obedient believer, an exhortation not to murmur against Allah's incomprehensible omnipotence. Khidr symbolizes not only the higher wisdom but also a way of acting which is in accord with this wisdom and transcends reason.

248   Anyone hearing such a mystery tale will recognize himself in the questing Moses and the forgetful Joshua, and the tale shows him how the immortality-bringing rebirth comes about. Characteristically, it is neither Moses nor Joshua who is transformed, but the forgotten fish. Where the fish disappears, there is the birthplace of Khidr. The immortal being issues from something humble and forgotten, indeed, from a wholly improbable source. This is the familiar motif of the hero's birth and need not be documented here. [18] Anyone who knows the Bible will think of Isaiah 53:2ff., where the "servant of God" is described, and of the gospel stories of the Nativity. The nourishing character of the transformative substance or deity is borne out by numerous cult-legends: Christ is the bread, Osiris the wheat,

---

17 Vollers, p. 254. This may possibly be due to Christian influence: one thinks of the fish meals of the early Christians and of fish symbolism in general. Vollers himself stresses the analogy between Christ and Khidr. Concerning the fish symbolism, see *Aion*.

18 Further examples in *Symbols of Transformation*, Part II. I could give many more from alchemy, but shall content myself with the old verse:

"This is the stone, poor and of little price,
Spurned by the fool, but honoured by the wise."

(*Ros. phil.*, in *Art. aurif.*, II, p. 210.) The "lapis exilis" may be a connecting-link with the "lapsit exillis," the grail of Wolfram von Eschenbach.

Mondamin the maize,[19] etc. These symbols coincide with a psychic fact which obviously, from the point of view of consciousness, has the significance merely of something to be assimilated, but whose real nature is overlooked. The fish symbol shows immediately what this is: it is the "nourishing" influence of unconscious contents, which maintain the vitality of consciousness by a continual influx of energy; for consciousness does not produce its energy by itself. What is capable of transformation is just this root of consciousness, which—inconspicuous and almost invisible (i.e., unconscious) though it is—provides consciousness with all its energy. Since the unconscious gives us the feeling that it is something alien, a non-ego, it is quite natural that it should be symbolized by an alien figure. Thus, on the one hand, it is the most insignificant of things, while on the other, so far as it potentially contains that "round" wholeness which consciousness lacks, it is the most significant of all. This "round" thing is the great treasure that lies hidden in the cave of the unconscious, and its personification is this personal being who represents the higher unity of conscious and unconscious. It is a figure comparable to Hiranyagarbha, Purusha, Atman, and the mystic Buddha. For this reason I have elected to call it the "self," by which I understand a psychic totality and at the same time a centre, neither of which coincides with the ego but includes it, just as a larger circle encloses a smaller one.

249   The intuition of immortality which makes itself felt during the transformation is connected with the peculiar nature of the unconscious. It is, in a sense, non-spatial and non-temporal. The empirical proof of this is the occurrence of so-called telepathic phenomena, which are still denied by hypersceptical critics, although in reality they are much more common than is generally supposed.[20] The feeling of immortality, it seems to me, has its origin in a peculiar feeling of extension in space and time, and I am inclined to regard the deification rites in the mysteries as a projection of this same psychic phenomenon.

250   The character of the self as a personality comes out very

---

[19] [The Ojibway legend of Mondamin was recorded by H. R. Schoolcraft and became a source for Longfellow's *Song of Hiawatha*. Cf. M. L. Williams, *Schoolcraft's Indian Legends*, pp. 58ff.—EDITORS.]

[20] Rhine, *New Frontiers of the Mind*. [Cf. also "Synchronicity: An Acausal Connecting Principle."—EDITORS.]

plainly in the Khidr legend. This feature is most strikingly expressed in the non-Koranic stories about Khidr, of which Vollers gives some telling examples. During my trip through Kenya, the headman of our safari was a Somali who had been brought up in the Sufi faith. To him Khidr was in every way a living person, and he assured me that I might at any time meet Khidr, because I was, as he put it, a *M'tu-ya-kitabu,*[21] a 'man of the Book,' meaning the Koran. He had gathered from our talks that I knew the Koran better than he did himself (which was, by the way, not saying a great deal). For this reason he regarded me as "islamu." He told me I might meet Khidr in the street in the shape of a man, or he might appear to me during the night as a pure white light, or—he smilingly picked a blade of grass—the Verdant One might even look like that. He said he himself had once been comforted and helped by Khidr, when he could not find a job after the war and was suffering want. One night, while he slept, he dreamt he saw a bright white light near the door and he knew it was Khidr. Quickly leaping to his feet (in the dream), he reverentially saluted him with the words *salem aleikum,* 'peace be with you,' and then he knew that his wish would be fulfilled. He added that a few days later he was offered the post as headman of a safari by a firm of outfitters in Nairobi.

251   This shows that, even in our own day, Khidr still lives on in the religion of the people, as friend, adviser, comforter, and teacher of revealed wisdom. The position assigned to him by dogma was, according to my Somali, that of *maleika kwanza-ya-mungu,* 'First Angel of God'—a sort of "Angel of the Face," an *angelos* in the true sense of the word, a messenger.

252   Khidr's character as a friend explains the subsequent part of the Eighteenth Sura, which reads as follows:

They will ask you about Dhulqarnein. Say: "I will give you an account of him.
"We made him mighty in the land and gave him means to achieve all things. He journeyed on a certain road until he reached the West and saw the sun setting in a pool of black mud. Hard by he found a certain people.

21 He spoke in Kiswahili, the lingua franca of East Africa. It contains many words borrowed from Arabic, as shown by the above example: *kitab* = book.

" 'Dhulqarnein,' We said, 'you must either punish them or show them kindness.'

"He replied: 'The wicked We shall surely punish. Then they shall return to their Lord and be sternly punished by Him. As for those that have faith and do good works, we shall bestow on them a rich reward and deal indulgently with them.'

"He then journeyed along another road until he reached the East and saw the sun rising upon a people whom We had utterly exposed to its flaming rays. So he did; and We had full knowledge of all the forces at his command.

"Then he followed yet another route until he came between the Two Mountains and found a people who could barely understand a word. 'Dhulqarnein,' they said, 'Gog and Magog are ravaging this land. Build us a rampart against them and we will pay you tribute.'

"He replied: 'The power which my Lord has given me is better than any tribute. Lend me a force of labourers, and I will raise a rampart between you and them. Come, bring me blocks of iron.'

"He dammed up the valley between the Two Mountains, and said: 'Ply your bellows.' And when the iron blocks were red with heat, he said: 'Bring me molten brass to pour on them.'

"Gog and Magog could not scale it, nor could they dig their way through it. He said: 'This is a blessing from my Lord. But when my Lord's promise is fulfilled, He will level it to dust. The promise of my Lord is true.' "

On that day We will let them come in tumultuous throngs. The Trumpet shall be sounded and We will gather them all together.

On that day Hell shall be laid bare before the unbelievers, who have turned a blind eye to My admonition and a deaf ear to My warning.

253   We see here another instance of that lack of coherence which is not uncommon in the Koran. How are we to account for this apparently abrupt transition to Dhulqarnein, the Two-horned One, that is to say, Alexander the Great? Apart from the unheard-of anachronism (Mohammed's chronology in general leaves much to be desired), one does not quite understand why Alexander is brought in here at all. But it has to be borne in mind that Khidr and Dhulqarnein are *the* great pair of friends, altogether comparable to the Dioscuri, as Vollers rightly emphasizes. The psychological connection may therefore be presumed to be as follows: Moses has had a profoundly moving experience of the self, which brought unconscious processes before his eyes

with overwhelming clarity. Afterwards, when he comes to his people, the Jews, who are counted among the infidels, and wants to tell them about his experience, he prefers to use the form of a mystery legend. Instead of speaking about himself, he speaks about the Two-horned One. Since Moses himself is also "horned," the substitution of Dhulqarnein appears plausible. Then he has to relate the history of this friendship and describe how Khidr helped his friend. Dhulqarnein makes his way to the setting of the sun and then to its rising. That is, he describes the way of the renewal of the sun, through death and darkness to a new resurrection. All this again indicates that it is Khidr who not only stands by man in his bodily needs but also helps him to attain rebirth.[22] The Koran, it is true, makes no distinction in this narrative between Allah, who is speaking in the first person plural, and Khidr. But it is clear that this section is simply a continuation of the helpful actions described previously, from which it is evident that Khidr is a symbolization or "incarnation" of Allah. The friendship between Khidr and Alexander plays an especially prominent part in the commentaries, as does also the connection with the prophet Elijah. Vollers does not hesitate to extend the comparison to that other pair of friends, Gilgamesh and Enkidu.[23]

254   To sum up, then: Moses has to recount the deeds of the two friends to his people in the manner of an impersonal mystery legend. Psychologically this means that the transformation has to be described or felt as happening to the "other." Although it is Moses himself who, in his experience with Khidr, stands in Dhulqarnein's place, he has to name the latter instead of himself in telling the story. This can hardly be accidental, for the great psychic danger which is always connected with individuation, or the development of the self, lies in the identification of ego-consciousness with the self. This produces an inflation which threatens consciousness with dissolution. All the more primitive or older cultures show a fine sense for the "perils of the soul" and for the dangerousness and general

---

[22] There are similar indications in the Jewish tales about Alexander. Cf. Bin Gorion, *Der Born Judas*, III, p. 133, for the legend of the "water of life," which is related to the 18th Sura.

[23] [For a fuller discussion of these relationships, see *Symbols of Transformation*, pars. 282ff.—EDITORS.]

unreliability of the gods. That is, they have not yet lost their psychic instinct for the barely perceptible and yet vital processes going on in the background, which can hardly be said of our modern culture. To be sure, we have before our eyes as a warning just such a pair of friends distorted by inflation—Nietzsche and Zarathustra—but the warning has not been heeded. And what are we to make of Faust and Mephistopheles? The Faustian hybris is already the first step towards madness. The fact that the unimpressive beginning of the transformation in *Faust* is a dog and not an edible fish, and that the transformed figure is the devil and not a wise friend, "endowed with Our grace and Our wisdom," might, I am inclined to think, offer a key to our understanding of the highly enigmatic Germanic soul.

255   Without entering into other details of the text, I would like to draw attention to one more point: the building of the rampart against Gog and Magog (also known as Yajuj and Majuj). This motif is a repetition of Khidr's last deed in the previous episode, the rebuilding of the town wall. But this time the wall is to be a strong defence against Gog and Magog. The passage may possibly refer to Revelation 20:7f. (AV):

And when the thousand years are expired, Satan shall be loosed out of his prison, and shall go out to deceive the nations which are in the four quarters of the earth, Gog and Magog, to gather them together for battle: the number of whom is as the sand of the sea. And they went up on the breadth of the earth, and compassed the camp of the saints about, and the beloved city.

256   Here Dhulqarnein takes over the role of Khidr and builds an unscalable rampart for the people living "between Two Mountains." This is obviously the same place in the middle which is to be protected against Gog and Magog, the featureless, hostile masses. Psychologically, it is again a question of the self, enthroned in the place of the middle, and referred to in Revelation as the beloved city (Jerusalem, the centre of the earth). The self is the hero, threatened already at birth by envious collective forces; the jewel that is coveted by all and arouses jealous strife; and finally the god who is dismembered by the old, evil power of darkness. In its psychological meaning, individuation is an *opus contra naturam*, which creates a *horror vacui* in the collective layer and is only too likely to collapse under the impact of

the collective forces of the psyche. The mystery legend of the two helpful friends promises protection [24] to him who has found the jewel on his quest. But there will come a time when, in accordance with Allah's providence, even the iron rampart will fall to pieces, namely, on the day when the world comes to an end, or psychologically speaking, when individual consciousness is extinguished in the waters of darkness, that is to say when a *subjective* end of the world is experienced. By this is meant the moment when consciousness sinks back into the darkness from which it originally emerged, like Khidr's island: the moment of death.

257 The legend then continues along eschatological lines: on that day (the day of the Last Judgment) the light returns to eternal light and the darkness to eternal darkness. The opposites are separated and a timeless state of permanence sets in, which, because of the absolute separation of opposites, is nevertheless one of supreme tension and therefore corresponds to the improbable initial state. This is in contrast to the view which sees the end as a *complexio oppositorum*.

258 With this prospect of eternity, Paradise, and Hell the Eighteenth Sura comes to an end. In spite of its apparently disconnected and allusive character, it gives an almost perfect picture of a psychic transformation or rebirth which today, with our greater psychological insight, we would recognize as an individuation process. Because of the great age of the legend and the Islamic prophet's primitive cast of mind, the process takes place entirely outside the sphere of consciousness and is projected in the form of a mystery legend of a friend or a pair of friends and the deeds they perform. That is why it is all so allusive and lacking in logical sequence. Nevertheless, the legend expresses the obscure archetype of transformation so admirably that the passionate religious *eros* of the Arab finds it completely satisfying. It is for this reason that the figure of Khidr plays such an important part in Islamic mysticism.

24 Just as the Dioscuri come to the aid of those who are in danger at sea.

III

THE PHENOMENOLOGY
OF THE SPIRIT IN FAIRYTALES

THE PHENOMENOLOGY OF THE SPIRIT
IN FAIRYTALES [1]

384   One of the unbreakable rules in scientific research is to take an object as known only so far as the inquirer is in a position to make scientifically valid statements about it. "Valid" in this sense simply means what can be verified by facts. The object of inquiry is the natural phenomenon. Now in psychology, one of the most important phenomena is the *statement,* and in particular its form and content, the latter aspect being perhaps the more significant with regard to the nature of the psyche. The first task that ordinarily presents itself is the description and arrangement of events, then comes the closer examination into the laws of their living behaviour. To inquire into the *substance* of what has been observed is possible in natural science only where there is an Archimedean point outside. For the psyche, no such outside standpoint exists—only the psyche can observe the psyche. Consequently, knowledge of the psychic substance is impossible for us, at least with the means at present available. This does not rule out the possibility that the atomic physics of the future may supply us with the said Archimedean point. For the time being, however, our subtlest lucubrations can establish no more than is expressed in the statement: this is how the psyche behaves. The honest investigator will piously refrain from meddling with questions of substance. I do not think it superfluous to acquaint my reader with the necessary limitations that psychology voluntarily imposes on itself, for he will then be in a position to appreciate the phenomenological standpoint of modern psychology, which is not always understood. This

1 [First published as a lecture, "Zur Psychologie des Geistes," in the *Eranos-Jahr-buch 1945.* Revised and published as "Zur Phänomenologie des Geistes im Märchen," in *Symbolik des Geistes* (Zurich, 1948), from which the present translation was made. This translation was published in a slightly different form in *Spirit and Nature* (Papers from the Eranos Yearbooks, 1; New York, 1953; London, 1954).—EDITORS.]

standpoint does not exclude the existence of faith, conviction, and experienced certainties of whatever description, nor does it contest their possible validity. Great as is their importance for the individual and for collective life, psychology completely lacks the means to prove their validity in the scientific sense. One may lament this incapacity on the part of science, but that does not enable it to jump over its own shadow.

I. CONCERNING THE WORD 'SPIRIT'

385   The word "spirit" possesses such a wide range of application that it requires considerable effort to make clear to oneself all the things it can mean. Spirit, we say, is the principle that stands in opposition to matter. By this we understand an immaterial substance or form of existence which on the highest and most universal level is called "God." We imagine this immaterial substance also as the vehicle of psychic phenomena or even of life itself. In contradiction to this view there stands the antithesis: spirit and nature. Here the concept of spirit is restricted to the supernatural or anti-natural, and has lost its substantial connection with psyche and life. A similar restriction is implied in Spinoza's view that spirit is an attribute of the One Substance. Hylozoism goes even further, taking spirit to be a quality of matter.

386   A very widespread view conceives spirit as a higher and psyche as a lower principle of activity, and conversely the alchemists thought of spirit as the *ligamentum animae et corporis*, obviously regarding it as a *spiritus vegetativus* (the later life-spirit or nerve-spirit). Equally common is the view that spirit and psyche are essentially the same and can be separated only arbitrarily. Wundt takes spirit as "the inner being, regardless of any connection with an outer being." Others restrict spirit to certain psychic capacities or functions or qualities, such as the capacity to think and reason in contradistinction to the more "soulful" sentiments. Here spirit means the sum-total of all the phenomena of rational thought, or of the intellect, including the will, memory, imagination, creative power, and aspirations motivated by ideals. Spirit has the further connotation of *sprightliness*, as when we say that a person is "spirited," mean-

ing that he is versatile and full of ideas, with a brilliant, witty, and surprising turn of mind. Again, spirit denotes a certain attitude or the principle underlying it, for instance, one is "educated in the spirit of Pestalozzi," or one says that the "spirit of Weimar is the immortal German heritage." A special instance is the time-spirit, or spirit of the age, which stands for the principle and motive force behind certain views, judgments, and actions of a collective nature. Then there is the "objective spirit," [2] by which is meant the whole stock of man's cultural possessions with particular regard to his intellectual and religious achievements.

387   As linguistic usage shows, spirit in the sense of an attitude has unmistakable leanings towards personification: the spirit of Pestalozzi can also be taken concretistically as his ghost or imago, just as the spirits of Weimar are the personal spectres of Goethe and Schiller; for spirit still has the spookish meaning of the soul of one departed. The "cold breath of the spirits" points on the one hand to the ancient affinity of ψυχή with ψυχρός and ψῦχος, which both mean 'cold,' and on the other hand to the original meaning of πνεῦμα, which simply denoted 'air in motion'; and in the same way animus and anima were connected with ἄνεμος, 'wind.' The German word *Geist* probably has more to do with something frothing, effervescing, or fermenting; hence affinities with *Gischt* (foam), *Gäscht* (yeast), *ghost*, and also with the emotional *ghastly* and *aghast*, are not to be rejected. From time immemorial emotion has been regarded as possession, which is why we still say today, of a hot-tempered person, that he is possessed of a devil or that an evil spirit has entered into him.[3] Just as, according to the old view, the spirits or souls of the dead are of a subtle disposition like a vapour or a smoke, so to the alchemist *spiritus* was a subtle, volatile, active, and vivifying essence, such as alcohol was understood to be, and all the arcane substances. On this level, spirit includes spirits of salts, spirits of ammonia, formic spirit, etc.

388   This score or so of meanings and shades of meaning attributable to the word "spirit" make it difficult for the psychologist to delimit his subject conceptually, but on the other hand they lighten the task of describing it, since the many different aspects

2 [An Hegelian term, roughly equivalent to our "spirit of man."—TRANS.]
3 See my "Spirit and Life."

go to form a vivid and concrete picture of the phenomenon in question. We are concerned with a functional complex which originally, on the primitive level, was felt as an invisible, breath-like "presence." William James has given us a lively account of this primordial phenomenon in his *Varieties of Religious Experience*. Another well-known example is the wind of the Pentecostal miracle. The primitive mentality finds it quite natural to personify the invisible presence as a ghost or demon. The souls or spirits of the dead are identical with the psychic activity of the living; they merely continue it. The view that the psyche is a spirit is implicit in this. When therefore something psychic happens in the individual which he feels as belonging to himself, that something is his own spirit. But if anything psychic happens which seems to him strange, then it is somebody else's spirit, and it may be causing a possession. The spirit in the first case corresponds to the subjective attitude, in the latter case to public opinion, to the time-spirit, or to the original, not yet human, anthropoid disposition which we also call the *unconscious*.

389   In keeping with its original wind-nature, spirit is always an active, winged, swift-moving being as well as that which vivifies, stimulates, incites, fires, and inspires. To put it in modern language, spirit is the dynamic principle, forming for that very reason the classical antithesis of matter—the antithesis, that is, of its stasis and inertia. Basically it is the contrast between life and death. The subsequent differentiation of this contrast leads to the actually very remarkable opposition of spirit and nature. Even though spirit is regarded as essentially alive and enlivening, one cannot really feel nature as unspiritual and dead. We must therefore be dealing here with the (Christian) postulate of a spirit whose life is so vastly superior to the life of nature that in comparison with it the latter is no better than death.

390   This special development in man's idea of spirit rests on the recognition that its invisible presence is a psychic phenomenon, i.e., one's own spirit, and that this consists not only of uprushes of life but of formal products too. Among the first, the most prominent are the images and shadowy presentations that occupy our inner field of vision; among the second, thinking and reason, which organize the world of images. In this way a tran-

scendent spirit superimposed itself upon the original, natural life-spirit and even swung over to the opposite position, as though the latter were merely naturalistic. The transcendent spirit became the supranatural and transmundane cosmic principle of order and as such was given the name of "God," or at least it became an attribute of the One Substance (as in Spinoza) or one Person of the Godhead (as in Christianity).

391   The corresponding development of spirit in the reverse, hylozoistic direction—*a maiori ad minus*—took place under anti-Christian auspices in materialism. The premise underlying this reaction is the exclusive certainty of the spirit's identity with psychic functions, whose dependence upon brain and metabolism became increasingly clear. One had only to give the One Substance another name and call it "matter" to produce the idea of a spirit which was entirely dependent on nutrition and environment, and whose highest form was the intellect or reason. This meant that the original pneumatic presence had taken up its abode in man's physiology, and a writer like Klages could arraign the spirit as the "adversary of the soul." [4] For it was into this latter concept that the original spontaneity of the spirit withdrew after it had been degraded to a servile attribute of matter. Somewhere or other the *deus ex machina* quality of spirit had to be preserved—if not in the spirit itself, then in its synonym the soul, that glancing, Aeolian [5] thing, elusive as a butterfly (anima, ψυχή).

392   Even though the materialistic conception of the spirit did not prevail everywhere, it still persisted, outside the sphere of religion, in the realm of conscious phenomena. Spirit as "subjective spirit" came to mean a purely endopsychic phenomenon, while "objective spirit" did not mean the universal spirit, or God, but merely the sum total of intellectual and cultural possessions which make up our human institutions and the content of our libraries. Spirit had forfeited its original nature, its autonomy and spontaneity over a very wide area, with the solitary exception of the religious field, where, at least in principle, its pristine character remained unimpaired.

[4] Ludwig Klages, *Der Geist als Widersacher der Seele*.
[5] *Soul*, from Old German *saiwalô*, may be cognate with αἰόλος, 'quick-moving, changeful of hue, shifting.' It also has the meaning of 'wily' or 'shifty'; hence an air of probability attaches to the alchemical definition of *anima* as Mercurius.

In this résumé we have described an entity which presents itself to us as an immediate psychic phenomenon distinguished from other psychisms whose existence is naïvely believed to be causally dependent upon physical influences. A connection between spirit and physical conditions is not immediately apparent, and for this reason it was credited with immateriality to a much higher degree than was the case with psychic phenomena in the narrower sense. Not only is a certain physical dependence attributed to the latter, but they are themselves thought of as possessing a kind of materiality, as the idea of the subtle body and the Chinese *kuei*-soul clearly show. In view of the intimate connection that exists between certain psychic processes and their physical parallels we cannot very well accept the total immateriality of the psyche. As against this, the *consensus omnium* insists on the immateriality of spirit, though not everyone would agree that it also has a reality of its own. It is, however, not easy to see why our hypothetical "matter," which looks quite different from what it did even thirty years ago, alone should be real, and spirit not. Although the idea of immateriality does not in itself exclude that of reality, popular opinion invariably associates reality with materiality. Spirit and matter may well be forms of one and the same transcendental being. For instance the Tantrists, with as much right, say that matter is nothing other than the concreteness of God's thoughts. The sole immediate reality is the psychic reality of conscious contents, which are as it were labelled with a spiritual or material origin as the case may be.

393   The hallmarks of spirit are, firstly, the principle of spontaneous movement and activity; secondly, the spontaneous capacity to produce images independently of sense perception; and thirdly, the autonomous and sovereign manipulation of these images. This spiritual entity approaches primitive man from outside; but with increasing development it gets lodged in man's consciousness and becomes a subordinate function, thus apparently forfeiting its original character of autonomy. That character is now retained only in the most conservative views, namely in the religions. The descent of spirit into the sphere of human consciousness is expressed in the myth of the divine νοῦς caught in the embrace of φύσις. This process, con-

tinuing over the ages, is probably an unavoidable necessity, and the religions would find themselves in a very forlorn situation if they believed in the attempt to hold up evolution. Their task, if they are well advised, is not to impede the ineluctable march of events, but to guide it in such a way that it can proceed without fatal injury to the soul. The religions should therefore constantly recall to us the origin and original character of the spirit, lest man should forget what he is drawing into himself and with what he is filling his consciousness. He himself did not create the spirit, rather the spirit makes *him* creative, always spurring him on, giving him lucky ideas, staying power, "enthusiasm" and "inspiration." So much, indeed, does it permeate his whole being that he is in gravest danger of thinking that he actually created the spirit and that he "has" it. In reality, however, the primordial phenomenon of the spirit takes possession of *him*, and, while appearing to be the willing object of human intentions, it binds his freedom, just as the physical world does, with a thousand chains and becomes an obsessive *idée-force*. Spirit threatens the naïve-minded man with inflation, of which our own times have given us the most horribly instructive examples. The danger becomes all the greater the more our interest fastens upon external objects and the more we forget that the differentiation of our relation to nature should go hand in hand with a correspondingly differentiated relation to the spirit, so as to establish the necessary balance. If the outer object is not offset by an inner, unbridled materialism results, coupled with maniacal arrogance or else the extinction of the autonomous personality, which is in any case the ideal of the totalitarian mass state.

394 As can readily be seen, the common modern idea of spirit ill accords with the Christian view, which regards it as the *summum bonum,* as God himself. To be sure, there is also the idea of an evil spirit. But the modern idea cannot be equated with that either, since for us spirit is not necessarily evil; we would have to call it morally indifferent or neutral. When the Bible says "God is spirit," it sounds more like the definition of a substance, or like a qualification. But the devil too, it seems, is endowed with the same peculiar spiritual substance, albeit an evil and corrupt one. The original identity of substance is

still expressed in the idea of the fallen angel, as well as in the
close connection between Jehovah and Satan in the Old Testament. There may be an echo of this primitive connection in the
Lord's Prayer, where we say "Lead us not into temptation"—
for is not this really the business of the *tempter,* the devil himself?

395   This brings us to a point we have not considered at all in the
course of our observations so far. We have availed ourselves of
cultural and everyday conceptions which are the product of
human consciousness and its reflections, in order to form a picture of the psychic modes of manifestation of the factor "spirit."
But we have yet to consider that because of its original autonomy,[6] about which there can be no doubt in the psychological
sense, the spirit is quite capable of staging its own manifestations spontaneously.

II. SELF-REPRESENTATION OF THE SPIRIT IN DREAMS

396   The psychic manifestations of the spirit indicate at once that
they are of an archetypal nature—in other words, the phenomenon we call spirit depends on the existence of an autonomous
primordial image which is universally present in the preconscious makeup of the human psyche. As usual, I first came up
against this problem when investigating the dreams of my patients. It struck me that a certain kind of father-complex has a
"spiritual" character, so to speak, in the sense that the father-
image gives rise to statements, actions, tendencies, impulses,
opinions, etc., to which one could hardly deny the attribute
"spiritual." In men, a positive father-complex very often produces a certain credulity with regard to authority and a distinct
willingness to bow down before all spiritual dogmas and values;
while in women, it induces the liveliest spiritual aspirations and
interests. In dreams, it is always the father-figure from whom
the decisive convictions, prohibitions, and wise counsels ema-

---

[6] Even if one accepts the view that a self-revelation of spirit—an apparition for
instance—is nothing but an hallucination, the fact remains that this is a spontaneous psychic event not subject to our control. At any rate it is an autonomous
complex, and that is quite sufficient for our purpose.

nate. The invisibility of this source is frequently emphasized by the fact that it consists simply of an authoritative voice which passes final judgments.[7] Mostly, therefore, it is the figure of a "wise old man" who symbolizes the spiritual factor. Sometimes the part is played by a "real" spirit, namely the ghost of one dead, or, more rarely, by grotesque gnomelike figures or talking animals. The dwarf forms are found, at least in my experience, mainly in women; hence it seems to me logical that in Ernst Barlach's play *Der tote Tag* (1912), the gnomelike figure of Steissbart ("Rumpbeard") is associated with the mother, just as Bes is associated with the mother-goddess at Karnak. In both sexes the spirit can also take the form of a boy or a youth. In women he corresponds to the so-called "positive" animus who indicates the possibility of conscious spiritual effort. In men his meaning is not so simple. He can be positive, in which case he signifies the "higher" personality, the self or *filius regius* as conceived by the alchemists.[8] But he can also be negative, and then he signifies the infantile shadow.[9] In both cases the boy means some form of spirit.[10] Graybeard and boy belong together. The pair of them play a considerable role in alchemy as symbols of Mercurius.

397   It can never be established with one-hundred-per-cent certainty whether the spirit-figures in dreams are morally good. Very often they show all the signs of duplicity, if not of outright malice. I must emphasize, however, that the grand plan on which the unconscious life of the psyche is constructed is so inaccessible to our understanding that we can never know what evil may not be necessary in order to produce good by enantiodromia, and what good may very possibly lead to evil. Sometimes the *probate spiritus* recommended by John cannot, with the best will in the world, be anything other than a cautious and patient waiting to see how things will finally turn out.

398   The figure of the wise old man can appear so plastically, not only in dreams but also in visionary meditation (or what we call

7 Cf. *Psychology and Alchemy*, par. 115.

8 Cf. the vision of the "naked boy" in Meister Eckhart (trans. by Evans, I, p. 438).

9 I would remind the reader of the "boys" in Bruno Goetz's novel *Das Reich ohne Raum*.

10 Cf. the paper on the "Child Archetype" in this volume, pars. 268f.

"active imagination"), that, as is sometimes apparently the case in India, it takes over the role of a guru.[11] The wise old man appears in dreams in the guise of a magician, doctor, priest, teacher, professor, grandfather, or any other person possessing authority. The archetype of spirit in the shape of a man, hobgoblin, or animal always appears in a situation where insight, understanding, good advice, determination, planning, etc., are needed but cannot be mustered on one's own resources. The archetype compensates this state of spiritual deficiency by contents designed to fill the gap. An excellent example of this is the dream about the white and black magicians, which tried to compensate the spiritual difficulties of a young theological student. I did not know the dreamer myself, so the question of my personal influence is ruled out. He dreamed *he was standing in the presence of a sublime hieratic figure called the "white magician," who was nevertheless clothed in a long black robe. This magician had just ended a lengthy discourse with the words "And for that we require the help of the black magician." Then the door suddenly opened and another old man came in, the "black magician," who however was dressed in a white robe. He too looked noble and sublime. The black magician evidently wanted to speak with the white, but hesitated to do so in the presence of the dreamer. At that the white magician, pointing to the dreamer, said, "Speak, he is an innocent." So the black magician began to relate a strange story of how he had found the lost keys of Paradise and did not know how to use them. He had, he said, come to the white magician for an explanation of the secret of the keys. He told him that the king of the country in which he lived was seeking a suitable tomb for himself. His subjects had chanced to dig up an old sarcophagus containing the mortal remains of a virgin. The king opened the sarcophagus, threw away the bones, and had the empty sarcophagus buried again for later use. But no sooner had the bones seen the light of day than the being to whom they once had belonged*

---

[11] Hence the many miraculous stories about rishis and mahatmas. A cultured Indian with whom I once conversed on the subject of gurus told me, when I asked him who his guru had been, that it was Shankaracharya (who lived in the 8th and 9th cents.) "But that's the celebrated commentator," I remarked in amazement. Whereupon he replied, "Yes, so he was; but naturally it was his spirit," not in the least perturbed by my Western bewilderment.

—the virgin—changed into a black horse that galloped off into the desert. The black magician pursued it across the sandy wastes and beyond, and there after many vicissitudes and difficulties he found the lost keys of Paradise. That was the end of his story, and also, unfortunately, of the dream.

399 Here the compensation certainly did not fall out as the dreamer would wish, by handing him a solution on a plate; rather it confronted him with a problem to which I have already alluded, and one which life is always bringing us up against: namely, the uncertainty of all moral valuation, the bewildering interplay of good and evil, and the remorseless concatenation of guilt, suffering, and redemption. This path to the primordial religious experience is the right one, but how many can recognize it? It is like a still small voice, and it sounds from afar. It is ambiguous, questionable, dark, presaging danger and hazardous adventure; a razor-edged path, to be trodden for God's sake only, without assurance and without sanction.

III. THE SPIRIT IN FAIRYTALES

400 I would gladly present the reader with some more modern dream-material, but I fear that the individualism of dreams would make too high a demand upon our exposition and would claim more space than is here at our disposal. We shall therefore turn to folklore, where we need not get involved in the grim confrontations and entanglements of individual case histories and can observe the variations of the spirit motif without having to consider conditions that are more or less unique. In myths and fairytales, as in dreams, the psyche tells its own story, and the interplay of the archetypes is revealed in its natural setting as "formation, transformation / the eternal Mind's eternal recreation."

401 The frequency with which the spirit-type appears as an old man is about the same in fairytales as in dreams.[12] The old man always appears when the hero is in a hopeless and desperate situation from which only profound reflection or a lucky idea —in other words, a spiritual function or an endopsychic autom-

12 I am indebted to Mrs. H. von Roques and Dr. Marie-Louise von Franz for the fairytale material used here.

atism of some kind—can extricate him. But since, for internal and external reasons, the hero cannot accomplish this himself, the knowledge needed to compensate the deficiency comes in the form of a personified thought, i.e., in the shape of this sagacious and helpful old man. An Estonian fairytale,[13] for instance, tells how an ill-treated little orphan boy who had let a cow escape was afraid to return home again for fear of more punishment. So he ran away, chancing to luck. He naturally got himself into a hopeless situation, with no visible way out. Exhausted, he fell into a deep sleep. When he awoke, "it seemed to him that he had something liquid in his mouth, and he saw a little old man with a long grey beard standing before him, who was in the act of replacing the stopper in his little milk-flask. 'Give me some more to drink,' begged the boy. 'You have had enough for today,' replied the old man. 'If my path had not chanced to lead me to you, that would assuredly have been your last sleep, for when I found you, you were half dead.' Then the old man asked the boy who he was and where he wanted to go. The boy recounted everything he could remember happening to him up to the beating he had received the previous evening. 'My dear child,' said the old man, 'you are no better and no worse off than many others whose dear protectors and comforters rest in their coffins under the earth. You can no longer turn back. Now that you have run away, you must seek a new fortune in the world. As I have neither house nor home, nor wife nor child, I cannot take further care of you, but I will give you some good advice for nothing.'"

402   So far the old man has been expressing no more than what the boy, the hero of the tale, could have thought out for himself. Having given way to the stress of emotion and simply run off like that into the blue, he would at least have had to reflect that he needed food. It would also have been necessary, at such a moment, to consider his position. The whole story of his life up to the recent past would then have passed before his mind, as is usual in such cases. An anamnesis of this kind is a purpose-

13 *Finnische und estnische Volksmärchen*, No. 68, p. 208 ["How an Orphan Boy Unexpectedly Found His Luck"]. [All German collections of tales here cited are listed under "Folktales" in the bibliography, q.v. English titles of tales are given in brackets, though no attempt has been made to locate published translations. —EDITORS.]

ful process whose aim is to gather the assets of the whole personality together at the critical moment, when all one's spiritual and physical forces are challenged, and with this united strength to fling open the door of the future. No one can help the boy to do this; he has to rely entirely on himself. There is no going back. This realization will give the necessary resolution to his actions. By forcing him to face the issue, the old man saves him the trouble of making up his mind. Indeed the old man is himself this purposeful reflection and concentration of moral and physical forces that comes about spontaneously in the psychic space outside consciousness when conscious thought is not yet—or is no longer—possible. The concentration and tension of psychic forces have something about them that always looks like magic: they develop an unexpected power of endurance which is often superior to the conscious effort of will. One can observe this experimentally in the artificial concentration induced by hypnosis: in my demonstrations I used regularly to put an hysteric, of weak bodily build, into a deep hypnotic sleep and then get her to lie with the back of her head on one chair and her heels resting on another, stiff as a board, and leave her there for about a minute. Her pulse would gradually go up to 90. A husky young athlete among the students tried in vain to imitate this feat with a conscious effort of will. He collapsed in the middle with his pulse racing at 120.

403   When the clever old man had brought the boy to this point he could begin his good advice, i.e., the situation no longer looked hopeless. He advised him to continue his wanderings, always to the eastward, where after seven years he would reach the great mountain that betokened his good fortune. The bigness and tallness of the mountain are allusions to his adult personality.[14] Concentration of his powers brings assurance and is therefore the best guarantee of success.[15] From now on he will

14 The mountain stands for the goal of the pilgrimage and ascent, hence it often has the psychological meaning of the self. The I Ching describes the goal thus: "The king introduces him / To the Western Mountain" (Wilhelm/Baynes trans., 1967, p. 74—Hexagram 17, Sui, "Following"). Cf. Honorius of Autun (Expositio in Cantica canticorum, col. 389): "The mountains are prophets." Richard of St. Victor says: "Vis videre Christum transfiguratum? Ascende in montem istum, disce cognoscere te ipsum" (Do you wish to see the transfigured Christ? Ascend that mountain and learn to know yourself). (Benjamin minor, cols. 53-56.)

15 In this respect we would call attention to the phenomenology of yoga.

lack for nothing. "Take my scrip and my flask," says the old man, "and each day you will find in them all the food and drink you need." At the same time he gave him a burdock leaf that could change into a boat whenever the boy had to cross water.

404   Often the old man in fairytales asks questions like who? why? whence? and whither?[16] for the purpose of inducing self-reflection and mobilizing the moral forces, and more often still he gives the necessary magical talisman,[17] the unexpected and improbable power to succeed, which is one of the peculiarities of the unified personality in good or bad alike. But the intervention of the old man—the spontaneous objectivation of the archetype—would seem to be equally indispensable, since the conscious will by itself is hardly ever capable of uniting the personality to the point where it acquires this extraordinary power to succeed. For that, not only in fairytales but in life generally, the objective intervention of the archetype is needed, which checks the purely affective reactions with a chain of inner confrontations and realizations. These cause the who? where? how? why? to emerge clearly and in this wise bring knowledge of the immediate situation as well as of the goal. The resultant enlightenment and untying of the fatal tangle often has something positively magical about it—an experience not unknown to the psychotherapist.

405   The tendency of the old man to set one thinking also takes the form of urging people to "sleep on it." Thus he says to the girl who is searching for her lost brothers: "Lie down:

16 There are numerous examples of this: *Spanische und Portugiesische Volksmärchen*, pp. 158, 199 ["The White Parrot" and "Queen Rose, or Little Tom"]; *Russische Volksmärchen*, p. 149 ["The Girl with No Hands"]; *Balkanmärchen*, p. 64 ["The Shepherd and the Three Samovilas (Nymphs)"]; *Märchen aus Iran*, pp. 150ff. ["The Secret of the Bath of Windburg"]; *Nordische Volksmärchen*, I, p. 231 ["The Werewolf"].

17 To the girl looking for her brothers he gives a ball of thread that rolls towards them (*Finnische und Estnische Volksmärchen*, p. 260 ["The Contending Brothers"]). The prince who is searching for the kingdom of heaven is given a boat that goes by itself (*Deutsche Märchen seit Grimm*, pp. 381f. ["The Iron Boots"]). Other gifts are a flute that sets everybody dancing (*Balkanmärchen*, p. 173 ["The Twelve Crumbs"]), or the path-finding ball, the staff of invisibility (*Nordische Volksmärchen*, I, p. 97 ["The Princess with Twelve Pairs of Golden Shoes"]), miraculous dogs (ibid., p. 287 ["The Three Dogs"]), or a book of secret wisdom (*Chinesische Volksmärchen*, p. 258 ["Jang Liang"]).

morning is cleverer than evening." [18] He also sees through the gloomy situation of the hero who has got himself into trouble, or at least can give him such information as will help him on his journey. To this end he makes ready use of animals, particularly birds. To the prince who has gone in search of the kingdom of heaven the old hermit says: "I have lived here for three hundred years, but never yet has anybody asked me about the kingdom of heaven. I cannot tell you myself; but up there, on another floor of the house, live all kinds of birds, and they can surely tell you." [19] The old man knows what roads lead to the goal and points them out to the hero.[20] He warns of dangers to come and supplies the means of meeting them effectively. For instance, he tells the boy who has gone to fetch the silver water that the well is guarded by a lion who has the deceptive trick of sleeping with his eyes open and watching with his eyes shut;[21] or he counsels the youth who is riding to a magic fountain in order to fetch the healing draught for the king, only to draw the water at a trot because of the lurking witches who lasso everybody that comes to the fountain.[22] He charges the princess whose lover has been changed into a werewolf to make a fire and put a cauldron of tar over it. Then she must plunge her beloved white lily into the boiling tar, and when the werewolf comes, she must empty the cauldron over its head, which will release her lover from the spell.[23] Occasionally the old man is a very critical old man, as in the Caucasian tale of the youngest prince who wanted to build a flawless church for his father, so as to inherit the kingdom. This he does, and nobody can discover a single flaw, but then an old man comes along and says, "That's a fine church you've built, to be sure! What a pity the main wall is a bit crooked!" The prince has the church pulled down again

---

18 *Finnische und estnische Volksmärchen,* loc. cit.

19 *Deutsche Märchen seit Grimm,* p. 382 [op. cit.]. In one Balkan tale (*Balkanmärchen,* p. 65 ["The Shepherd and the Three Samovilas"]) the old man is called the "Czar of all the birds." Here the magpie knows all the answers. Cf. the mysterious "master of the dovecot" in Gustav Meyrink's novel *Der weisse Dominikaner.*

20 *Märchen aus Iran,* p. 152 [op. cit.].

21 *Spanische und Portugiesische Märchen,* p. 158 ["The White Parrot"].

22 *Ibid.,* p. 199 ["Queen Rose, or Little Tom"].

23 *Nordische Volksmärchen,* Vol. I, p. 231f. ["The Werewolf"].

and builds a new one, but here too the old man discovers a flaw, and so on for the third time.[24]

406   The old man thus represents knowledge, reflection, insight, wisdom, cleverness, and intuition on the one hand, and on the other, moral qualities such as goodwill and readiness to help, which make his "spiritual" character sufficiently plain. Since the archetype is an autonomous content of the unconscious, the fairytale, which usually concretizes the archetypes, can cause the old man to appear in a dream in much the same way as happens in modern dreams. In a Balkan tale the old man appears to the hard-pressed hero in a dream and gives him good advice about accomplishing the impossible tasks that have been imposed upon him.[25] His relation to the unconscious is clearly expressed in one Russian fairytale, where he is called the "King of the Forest." As the peasant sat down wearily on a tree stump, a little old man crept out: "all wrinkled he was and a green beard hung down to his knees." "Who are you?" asked the peasant. "I am Och, King of the Forest," said the manikin. The peasant hired out his profligate son to him, "and the King of the Forest departed with the young man, and conducted him to that other world under the earth and brought him to a green hut. . . . In the hut everything was green: the walls were green and the benches, Och's wife was green and the children were green . . . and the little water-women who waited on him were as green as rue." Even the food was green. The King of the Forest is here a vegetation or tree numen who reigns in the woods and, through the nixies, also has connections with water, which clearly shows his relation to the unconscious since the latter is frequently expressed through wood and water symbols.

407   There is equally a connection with the unconscious when the old man appears as a dwarf. The fairytale about the princess who was searching for her lover says: "Night came and the darkness, and still the princess sat in the same place and wept. As she sat there lost in thought, she heard a voice greeting her: 'Good evening, pretty maid! Why are you sitting here so lonely and sad?' She sprang up hastily and felt very confused, and that was no wonder. But when she looked round there was only a tiny little old man standing before her, who nodded his head at her

[24] *Kaukasische Märchen*, pp. 35f. ["The False and the True Nightingale"].
[25] *Balkanmärchen*, p. 217 ["The Lubi (She-Devil) and the Fair of the Earth"].

and looked so kind and simple." In a Swiss fairytale, the peasant's son who wants to bring the king's daughter a basket of apples encounters "es chlis isigs Männdli, das frogt-ne, was er do i dem Chratte häig?" (a little iron man who asked what he had there in the basket). In another passage the "Männdli" has "es isigs Chlaidli a" (iron clothes on). By "isig" presumably "eisern" (iron) is meant, which is more probable than "eisig" (icy). In the latter case it would have to be "es Chlaidli vo Is" (clothes of ice).[26] There are indeed little ice men, and little metal men too; in fact, in a modern dream I have even come across a little black iron man who appeared at a critical juncture, like the one in this fairytale of the country bumpkin who wanted to marry the princess.

408   In a modern series of visions in which the figure of the wise old man occurred several times, he was on one occasion of normal size and appeared at the very bottom of a crater surrounded by high rocky walls; on another occasion he was a tiny figure on the top of a mountain, inside a low, stony enclosure. We find the same motif in Goethe's tale of the dwarf princess who lived in a casket.[27] In this connection we might also mention the Anthroparion, the little leaden man of the Zosimos vision,[28] as well as the metallic men who dwell in the mines, the crafty dactyls of antiquity, the homunculi of the alchemists, and the gnomic throng of hobgoblins, brownies, gremlins, etc. How "real" such conceptions are became clear to me on the occasion of a serious mountaineering accident: after the catastrophe two of the climbers had the collective vision, in broad daylight, of a little hooded man who scrambled out of an inaccessible crevasse in the ice face and passed across the glacier, creating a regular panic in the two beholders. I have often encountered motifs which made me think that the unconscious must be the world of the infinitesimally small. Such an idea could be derived rationalistically from the obscure feeling that in all these visions we are dealing with something endopsychic, the inference being that a thing must be exceedingly small in order to fit

---

[26] This occurs in the tale of the griffin, No. 84 in the volume of children's fairy-tales collected by the brothers Grimm (1912), II, pp. 84ff. The text swarms with phonetic mistakes. [The English text (trans. by Margaret Hunt, rev. by James Stern, no. 165) has "hoary."—TRANS.]   [27] Goethe, "Die neue Melusine."
[28] Cf. "The Visions of Zosimos," par. 87 (III, i, 2–3).

inside the head. I am no friend of any such "rational" conjectures, though I would not say that they are all beside the mark. It seems to me more probable that this liking for diminutives on the one hand and for superlatives—giants, etc.—on the other is connected with the queer uncertainty of spatial and temporal relations in the unconscious.[29] Man's sense of proportion, his rational conception of big and small, is distinctly anthropomorphic, and it loses its validity not only in the realm of physical phenomena but also in those parts of the collective unconscious beyond the range of the specifically human. The atman is "smaller than small and bigger than big," he is "the size of a thumb" yet he "encompasses the earth on every side and rules over the ten-finger space." And of the Cabiri Goethe says: "little in length / mighty in strength." In the same way, the archetype of the wise old man is quite tiny, almost imperceptible, and yet it possesses a fateful potency, as anyone can see when he gets down to fundamentals. The archetypes have this peculiarity in common with the atomic world, which is demonstrating before our eyes that the more deeply the investigator penetrates into the universe of microphysics the more devastating are the explosive forces he finds enchained there. That the greatest effects come from the smallest causes has become patently clear not only in physics but in the field of psychological research as well. How often in the critical moments of life everything hangs on what appears to be a mere nothing!

409   In certain primitive fairytales, the illuminating quality of our archetype is expressed by the fact that the old man is identified with the sun. He brings a firebrand with him which he uses for roasting a pumpkin. After he has eaten, he takes the fire away again, which causes mankind to steal it from him.[30] In a North American Indian tale, the old man is a witch-doctor who owns the fire.[31] Spirit too has a fiery aspect, as we know from the language of the Old Testament and from the story of the Pentecostal miracle.

---

29 In one Siberian fairytale (*Märchen aus Sibirien*, no. 13 ["The Man Turned to Stone"]) the old man is a white shape towering up to heaven.
30 *Indianermärchen aus Südamerika*, p. 285 ["The End of the World and the Theft of Fire"—Bolivian].
31 *Indianermärchen aus Nordamerika*, p. 74 [Tales of Manabos: "The Theft of Fire"].

410   Apart from his cleverness, wisdom, and insight, the old man, as we have already mentioned, is also notable for his moral qualities; what is more, he even tests the moral qualities of others and makes his gifts dependent on this test. There is a particularly instructive example of this in the Estonian fairytale of the stepdaughter and the real daughter. The former is an orphan distinguished for her obedience and good behaviour. The story begins with her distaff falling into a well. She jumps in after it, but does not drown, and comes to a magic country where, continuing her quest, she meets a cow, a ram, and an appletree whose wishes she fulfils. She now comes to a washhouse where a dirty old man is sitting who wants her to wash him. The following dialogue develops: "Pretty maid, pretty maid, wash me, do, it is hard for me to be so dirty!" "What shall I heat the stove with?" "Collect wooden pegs and crows' dung and make a fire with that." But she fetches sticks, and asks, "Where shall I get the bath-water?" "Under the barn there stands a white mare. Get her to piss into the tub!" But she takes clean water, and asks, "Where shall I get a bath-switch?" "Cut off the white mare's tail and make a bath-switch of that!" But she makes one out of birch-twigs, and asks, "Where shall I get soap?" "Take a pumice-stone and scrub me with that!" But she fetches soap from the village and with that she washes the old man.

411   As a reward he gives her a bag full of gold and precious stones. The daughter of the house naturally becomes jealous, throws her distaff into the well, where she finds it again instantly. Nevertheless she goes on and does everything wrong that the stepdaughter had done right, and is rewarded accordingly. The frequency of this motif makes further examples superfluous.

412   The figure of the superior and helpful old man tempts one to connect him somehow or other with God. In the German tale of the soldier and the black princess [32] it is related how the princess, on whom a curse has been laid, creeps out of her iron coffin every night and devours the soldier standing guard over the tomb. One soldier, when his turn came, tried to escape. "That evening he stole away, fled over the fields and mountains,

32 *Deutsche Märchen seit Grimm,* pp. 189ff.

and came to a beautiful meadow. Suddenly a little man stood before him with a long grey beard, but it was none other than the Lord God himself, who could no longer go on looking at all the mischief the devil wrought every night. 'Whither away?' said the little grey man, 'may I come with you?' And because the little old man looked so friendly the soldier told him that he had run away and why he had done so." Good advice follows, as always. In this story the old man is taken for God in the same naïve way that the English alchemist, Sir George Ripley,[33] describes the "old king" as "antiquus dierum"—"the Ancient of Days."

413   Just as all archetypes have a positive, favourable, bright side that points upwards, so also they have one that points downwards, partly negative and unfavourable, partly chthonic, but for the rest merely neutral. To this the spirit archetype is no exception. Even his dwarf form implies a kind of limitation and suggests a naturalistic vegetation-numen sprung from the underworld. In one Balkan tale, the old man is handicapped by the loss of an eye. It has been gouged out by the Vili, a species of winged demon, and the hero is charged with the task of getting them to restore it to him. The old man has therefore lost part of his eyesight—that is, his insight and enlightenment—to the daemonic world of darkness; this handicap is reminiscent of the fate of Osiris, who lost an eye at the sight of a black pig (his wicked brother Set), or again of Wotan, who sacrificed his eye at the spring of Mimir. Characteristically enough, the animal ridden by the old man in our fairytale is a goat, a sign that he himself has a dark side. In a Siberian tale, he appears as a one-legged, one-handed, and one-eyed greybeard who wakens a dead man with an iron staff. In the course of the story the latter, after being brought back to life several times, kills the old man by a mistake, and thus throws away his good fortune. The story is entitled "The One-sided Old Man," and in truth his handicap shows that he consists of one half only. The other half is invisible, but appears in the shape of a murderer who seeks the hero's life. Eventually the hero succeeds in killing his persistent murderer, but in the struggle he also kills the one-sided old man, so that the identity of the two victims is clearly revealed. It is thus possible that the old man is his own opposite, a life-

33 In his "Cantilena" (15 cent.). [Cf. *Mysterium Coniunctionis*, par. 374.]

bringer as well as a death-dealer—"ad utrumque peritus" (skilled in both), as is said of Hermes.[34]

414   In these circumstances, whenever the "simple" and "kindly" old man appears, it is advisable for heuristic and other reasons to scrutinize the context with some care. For instance, in the Estonian tale we first mentioned, about the hired boy who lost the cow, there is a suspicion that the helpful old man who happened to be on the spot so opportunely had surreptitiously made away with the cow beforehand in order to give his protégé an excellent reason for taking to flight. This may very well be, for everyday experience shows that it is quite possible for a superior, though subliminal, foreknowledge of fate to contrive some annoying incident for the sole purpose of bullying our Simple Simon of an ego-consciousness into the way he should go, which for sheer stupidity he would never have found by himself. Had our orphan guessed that it was the old man who had whisked off his cow as if by magic, he would have seemed like a spiteful troll or a devil. And indeed the old man has a wicked aspect too, just as the primitive medicine-man is a healer and helper and also the dreaded concocter of poisons. The very word φάρμαχον means 'poison' as well as 'antidote,' and poison can in fact be both.

415   The old man, then, has an ambiguous elfin character—witness the extremely instructive figure of Merlin—seeming, in certain of his forms, to be good incarnate and in others an aspect of evil. Then again, he is the wicked magician who, from sheer egoism, does evil for evil's sake. In a Siberian fairytale, he is an evil spirit "on whose head were two lakes with two ducks swimming in them." He feeds on human flesh. The story relates how the hero and his companions go to a feast in the next village, leaving their dogs at home. These, acting on the principle "when the cat's away the mice do play," also arrange a feast, at the climax of which they all hurl themselves on the stores of meat. The men return home and chase out the dogs, who dash off into the wilderness. "Then the Creator spoke to Ememqut [the hero of the tale]: 'Go and look for the dogs with your wife.'" But he gets caught in a terrible snow-storm and has to seek shelter in the hut of the evil spirit. There now follows the

---

34 Prudentius, *Contra Symmachum*, I, 94 (trans. by Thompson, I, p. 356). See Hugo Rahner, "Die seelenheilende Blume.'

well-known motif of the biter bit. The "Creator" is Ememqut's father, but the father of the Creator is called the "Self-created" because he created himself. Although we are nowhere told that the old man with the two lakes on his head lured the hero and his wife into the hut in order to satisfy his hunger, it may be conjectured that a very peculiar spirit must have got into the dogs to cause them to celebrate a feast like the men and after-wards—contrary to their nature—to run away, so that Ememqut had to go out and look for them; and that the hero was then caught in a snow-storm in order to drive him into the arms of the wicked old man. The fact that the Creator, son of the Self-created, was a party to the advice raises a knotty problem whose solution we had best leave to the Siberian theologians.

416   In a Balkan fairytale the old man gives the childless Czarina a magic apple to eat, from which she becomes pregnant and bears a son, it being stipulated that the old man shall be his godfather. The boy, however, grows up into a horrid little tough who bullies all the children and slaughters the cattle. For ten years he is given no name. Then the old man appears, sticks a knife into his leg, and calls him the "Knife Prince." The boy now wants to set forth on his adventures, which his father, after long hesitation, finally allows him to do. The knife in his leg is of vital importance: if he draws it out himself, he will live; if anybody else does so, he will die. In the end the knife becomes his doom, for an old witch pulls it out when he is asleep. He dies, but is restored to life by the friends he has won.[35] Here the old man is a helper, but also the contriver of a dangerous fate which might just as easily have turned out for the bad. The evil showed itself early and plainly in the boy's villainous character.

417   In another Balkan tale, there is a variant of our motif that is worth mentioning: A king is looking for his sister who has been abducted by a stranger. His wanderings bring him to the hut of an old woman, who warns him against continuing the search. But a tree laden with fruit, ever receding before him, lures him away from the hut. When at last the tree comes to a halt, an old man climbs down from the branches. He regales the king and takes him to a castle, where the sister is living with the old man as his wife. She tells her brother that the old man is a wicked

[35] *Balkanmärchen*, pp. 34ff. ["The Deeds of the Czar's Son and His Two Companions"].

spirit who will kill him. And sure enough, three days afterwards, the king vanishes without trace. His younger brother now takes up the search and kills the wicked spirit in the form of a dragon. A handsome young man is thereby released from the spell and forthwith marries the sister. The old man, appearing at first as a tree-numen, is obviously connected with the sister. He is a murderer. In an interpolated episode, he is accused of enchanting a whole city by turning it to iron, i.e., making it immovable, rigid, and locked up.[36] He also holds the king's sister a captive and will not let her return to her relatives. This amounts to saying that the sister is animus-possessed. The old man is therefore to be regarded as her animus. But the manner in which the king is drawn into this possession, and the way he seeks for his sister, make us think that she has an anima significance for her brother. The fateful archetype of the old man has accordingly first taken possession of the king's anima—in other words, robbed him of the archetype of life which the anima personifies—and forced him to go in search of the lost charm, the "treasure hard to attain," thus making him the mythical hero, the higher personality who is an expression of the self. Meanwhile, the old man acts the part of the villain and has to be forcibly removed, only to appear at the end as the husband of the sister-anima, or more properly as the bridegroom of the soul, who celebrates the sacred incest that symbolizes the union of opposites and equals. This bold enantiodromia, a very common occurrence, not only signifies the rejuvenation and transformation of the old man, but hints at a secret inner relation of evil to good and vice versa.

418   So in this story we see the archetype of the old man in the guise of an evil-doer, caught up in all the twists and turns of an individuation process that ends suggestively with the *hieros gamos*. Conversely, in the Russian tale of the Forest King, he starts by being helpful and benevolent, but then refuses to let his hired boy go, so that the main episodes in the story deal with the boy's repeated attempts to escape from the clutches of the magician. Instead of the quest we have flight, which nonetheless appears to win the same reward as adventures valiantly sought, for in the end the hero marries the king's daughter. The

36 Ibid., pp. 177ff. ["The Son-in-Law from Abroad"].

magician, however, must rest content with the role of the biter bit.

IV. THERIOMORPHIC SPIRIT SYMBOLISM IN FAIRYTALES

419   The description of our archetype would not be complete if we omitted to consider one special form of its manifestation, namely its animal form. This belongs essentially to the theriomorphism of gods and demons and has the same psychological significance. The animal form shows that the contents and functions in question are still in the extrahuman sphere, i.e., on a plane beyond human consciousness, and consequently have a share on the one hand in the daemonically superhuman and on the other in the bestially subhuman. It must be remembered, however, that this division is only true within the sphere of consciousness, where it is a necessary condition of thought. Logic says *tertium non datur,* meaning that we cannot envisage the opposites in their oneness. In other words, while the abolition of an obstinate antinomy can be no more than a postulate for us, this is by no means so for the unconscious, whose contents are without exception paradoxical or antinomial by nature, not excluding the category of being. If anyone unacquainted with the psychology of the unconscious wants to get a working knowledge of these matters, I would recommend a study of Christian mysticism and Indian philosophy, where he will find the clearest elaboration of the antinomies of the unconscious.

420   Although the old man has, up to now, looked and behaved more or less like a human being, his magical powers and his spiritual superiority suggest that, in good and bad alike, he is outside, or above, or below the human level. Neither for the primitive nor for the unconscious does his animal aspect imply any devaluation, for in certain respects the animal is superior to man. It has not yet blundered into consciousness nor pitted a self-willed ego against the power from which it lives; on the contrary, it fulfils the will that actuates it in a well-nigh perfect manner. Were it conscious, it would be morally better than man. There is deep doctrine in the legend of the fall: it is the expression of a dim presentiment that the emancipation of ego-consciousness was a Luciferian deed. Man's whole history con-

sists from the very beginning in a conflict between his feeling of inferiority and his arrogance. Wisdom seeks the middle path and pays for this audacity by a dubious affinity with daemon and beast, and so is open to moral misinterpretation.

421 Again and again in fairytales we encounter the motif of helpful animals. These act like humans, speak a human language, and display a sagacity and a knowledge superior to man's. In these circumstances we can say with some justification that the archetype of the spirit is being expressed through an animal form. A German fairytale [37] relates how a young man, while searching for his lost princess, meets a wolf, who says, "Do not be afraid! But tell me, where is your way leading you?" The young man recounts his story, whereupon the wolf gives him as a magic gift a few of his hairs, with which the young man can summon his help at any time. This intermezzo proceeds exactly like the meeting with the helpful old man. In the same story, the archetype also displays its other, wicked side. In order to make this clear I shall give a summary of the story:

422 While the young man is watching his pigs in the wood, he discovers a large tree, whose branches lose themselves in the clouds. "How would it be," says he to himself, "if you were to look at the world from the top of that great tree?" So he climbs up, all day long he climbs, without even reaching the branches. Evening comes, and he has to pass the night in a fork of the tree. Next day he goes on climbing and by noon has reached the foliage. Only towards evening does he come to a village nestling in the branches. The peasants who live there give him food and shelter for the night. In the morning he climbs still further. Towards noon, he reaches a castle in which a young girl lives. Here he finds that the tree goes no higher. She is a king's daughter, held prisoner by a wicked magician. So the young man stays with the princess, and she allows him to go into all the rooms of the castle: one room alone she forbids him to enter. But curiosity is too strong. He unlocks the door, and there in the room he finds a raven fixed to the wall with three nails. One nail goes through his throat, the two others through the wings. The raven complains of thirst and the young man, moved by pity, gives him water to drink. At each sip a nail falls out,

37 *Deutsche Märchen seit Grimm*, pp. 1ff. ["The Princess in the Tree"].

and at the third sip the raven is free and flies out at the window. When the princess hears of it she is very frightened and says, "That was the devil who enchanted me! It won't be long now before he fetches me again." And one fine morning she has indeed vanished.

423   The young man now sets out in search of her and, as we have described above, meets the wolf. In the same way he meets a bear and a lion, who also give him some hairs. In addition the lion informs him that the princess is imprisoned nearby in a hunting-lodge. The young man finds the house and the princess, but is told that flight is impossible, because the hunter possesses a three-legged white horse that knows everything and would infallibly warn its master. Despite that, the young man tries to flee away with her, but in vain. The hunter overtakes him but, because he had saved his life as a raven, lets him go and rides off again with the princess. When the hunter has disappeared into the wood, the young man creeps back to the house and persuades the princess to wheedle from the hunter the secret of how he obtained his clever white horse. This she successfully does in the night, and the young man, who has hidden himself under the bed, learns that about an hour's journey from the hunting-lodge there dwells a witch who breeds magic horses. Whoever was able to guard the foals for three days might choose a horse as a reward. In former times, said the hunter, she used to make a gift of twelve lambs into the bargain, in order to satisfy the hunger of the twelve wolves who lived in the woods near the farmstead, and prevent them from attacking; but to him she gave no lambs. So the wolves followed him as he rode away, and while crossing the borders of her domain they succeeded in tearing off one of his horse's hoofs. That was why it had only three legs.

424   Then the young man made haste to seek out the witch and agreed to serve her on condition that she gave him not only a horse of his own choosing but twelve lambs as well. To this she consented. Instantly she commanded the foals to run away, and, to make him sleepy, she gave him brandy. He drinks, falls asleep, and the foals escape. On the first day he catches them with the help of the wolf, on the second day the bear helps him, and on the third the lion. He can now go and choose his reward. The witch's little daughter tells him which horse her mother rides.

This is naturally the best horse, and it too is white. Hardly has he got it out of the stall when the witch pierces the four hoofs and sucks the marrow out of the bones. From this she bakes a cake and gives it to the young man for his journey. The horse grows deathly weak, but the young man feeds it on the cake, whereupon the horse recovers its former strength. He gets out of the woods unscathed after quieting the twelve wolves with the twelve lambs. He then fetches the princess and rides away with her. But the three-legged horse calls out to the hunter, who sets off in pursuit and quickly catches up with them, because the four-legged horse refuses to gallop. As the hunter approaches, the four-legged horse cries out to the three-legged, "Sister, throw him off!" The magician is thrown and trampled to pieces by the two horses. The young man sets the princess on the three-legged horse, and the pair of them ride away to her father's kingdom, where they get married. The four-legged horse begs him to cut off both their heads, for otherwise they would bring disaster upon him. This he does, and the horses are transformed into a handsome prince and a wonderfully beautiful princess, who after a while repair "to their own kingdom." They had been changed into horses by the hunter, long ago.

425   Apart from the theriomorphic spirit symbolism in this tale, it is especially interesting to note that the function of knowing and intuition is represented by a riding-animal. This is as much as to say that the spirit can be somebody's property. The three-legged white horse is thus the property of the demonic hunter, and the four-legged one the property of the witch. Spirit is here partly a function, which like any other object (horse) can change its owner, and partly an autonomous subject (magician as owner of the horse). By obtaining the four-legged horse from the witch, the young man frees a spirit or a thought of some special kind from the grip of the unconscious. Here as elsewhere, the witch stands for a *mater natura* or the original "matriarchal" state of the unconscious, indicating a psychic constitution in which the unconscious is opposed only by a feeble and still-dependent consciousness. The four-legged horse shows itself superior to the three-legged, since it can command the latter. And since the quaternity is a symbol of wholeness and wholeness plays a considerable role in the picture-world of the uncon-

scious,[38] the victory of four-leggedness over three-leggedness is not altogether unexpected. But what is the meaning of the opposition between threeness and fourness, or rather, what does threeness mean as compared with wholeness? In alchemy this problem is known as the axiom of Maria and runs all through alchemical philosophy for more than a thousand years, finally to be taken up again in the Cabiri scene in *Faust*. The earliest literary version of it is to be found in the opening words of Plato's *Timaeus*,[39] of which Goethe gives us a reminder. Among the alchemists we can see clearly how the divine Trinity has its counterpart in a lower, chthonic triad (similar to Dante's three-headed devil). This represents a principle which, by reason of its symbolism, betrays affinities with evil, though it is by no means certain that it expresses nothing but evil. Everything points rather to the fact that evil, or its familiar symbolism, belongs to the family of figures which describe the dark, nocturnal, lower, chthonic element. In this symbolism the lower stands to the higher as a correspondence [40] in reverse; that is to say it is conceived, like the upper, as a triad. Three, being a masculine number, is logically correlated with the wicked hunter, who can be thought of alchemically as the lower triad. Four, a feminine number, is assigned to the old woman. The two horses are miraculous animals that talk and know and thus represent the unconscious spirit, which in one case is subordinated to the wicked magician and in the other to the old witch.

426   Between the three and the four there exists the primary opposition of male and female, but whereas fourness is a symbol of wholeness, threeness is not. The latter, according to alchemy, denotes polarity, since one triad always presupposes another, just as high presupposes low, lightness darkness, good evil. In terms of energy, polarity means a potential, and wherever a

[38] With reference to the quaternity I would call attention to my earlier writings, and in particular to *Psychology and Alchemy* and "Psychology and Religion."

[39] The oldest representation I know of this problem is that of the four sons of Horus, three of whom are occasionally depicted with the heads of animals, and the other with the head of a man. Chronologically this links up with Ezekiel's vision of the four creatures, which then reappear in the attributes of the four evangelists. Three have animal heads and one a human head (the angel). [Cf. frontispiece to *Psychology and Religion: West and East.*—EDITORS.]

[40] According to the dictum in the "Tabula smaragdina," "Quod est inferius, est sicut quod est superius" (That which is below is like that which is above).

potential exists there is the possibility of a current, a flow of events, for the tension of opposites strives for balance. If one imagines the quaternity as a square divided into two halves by a diagonal, one gets two triangles whose apices point in opposite directions. One could therefore say metaphorically that if the wholeness symbolized by the quaternity is divided into equal halves, it produces two opposing triads. This simple reflection shows how three can be derived from four, and in the same way the hunter of the captured princess explains how his horse, from being four-legged, became three-legged, through having one hoof torn off by the twelve wolves. The three-leggedness is due to an accident, therefore, which occurred at the very moment when the horse was leaving the territory of the dark mother. In psychological language we should say that when the unconscious wholeness becomes manifest, i.e., leaves the unconscious and crosses over into the sphere of consciousness, one of the four remains behind, held fast by the *horror vacui* of the unconscious. There thus arises a triad, which as we know—not from the fairytale but from the history of symbolism—constellates a corresponding triad in opposition to it [41]—in other words, a conflict ensues. Here too we could ask with Socrates, "One, two, three—but, my dear Timaeus, of those who yesterday were the banqueters and today are the banquet-givers, where is the fourth?" [42] He has remained in the realm of the dark mother, caught by the wolfish greed of the unconscious, which is unwilling to let anything escape from its magic circle save at the cost of a sacrifice.

427   The hunter or old magician and the witch correspond to the negative parental imagos in the magic world of the unconscious. The hunter first appears in the story as a black raven. He has stolen away the princess and holds her a prisoner. She describes him as "the devil." But it is exceedingly odd that he himself is locked up in the one forbidden room of the castle and fixed to the wall with three nails, as though *crucified*. He is imprisoned, like all jailers, in his own prison, and bound like all who curse. The prison of both is a magic castle at the top of a gigantic tree, presumably the world-tree. The princess belongs to the upper

---

[41] Cf. *Psychology and Alchemy*, fig. 54 and par. 539; and, for a more detailed account, "The Spirit Mercurius," par. 271.
[42] This unexplained passage has been put down to Plato's "drollery."

region of light near the sun. Sitting there in captivity on the world-tree, she is a kind of *anima mundi* who has got herself into the power of darkness. But this catch does not seem to have done the latter much good either, seeing that the captor is crucified and moreover with three nails. The crucifixion evidently betokens a state of agonizing bondage and suspension, fit punishment for one foolhardy enough to venture like a Prometheus into the orbit of the opposing principle. This was what the raven, who is identical with the hunter, did when he ravished a precious soul from the upper world of light; and so, as a punishment, he is nailed to the wall in that upper world. That this is an inverted reflection of the primordial Christian image should be obvious enough. The Saviour who freed the soul of humanity from the dominion of the prince of this world was nailed to a cross down below on earth, just as the thieving raven is nailed to the wall in the celestial branches of the world-tree for his presumptuous meddling. In our fairytale, the peculiar instrument of the magic spell is the triad of nails. Who it was that made the raven captive is not told in the tale, but it sounds as if a spell had been laid upon him in the triune name.[43]

428   Having climbed up the world-tree and penetrated into the magic castle where he is to rescue the princess, our young hero is permitted to enter all the rooms but one, the very room in which the raven is imprisoned. Just as in paradise there was one tree of which it was forbidden to eat, so here there is one room that is not to be opened, with the natural result that it is entered at once. Nothing excites our interest more than a prohibition. It is the surest way of provoking disobedience. Obviously there is some secret scheme afoot to free not so much the princess as the raven. As soon as the hero catches sight of him, the raven begins to cry piteously and to complain of thirst,[44] and the

---

[43] In *Deutsche Märchen seit Grimm* (I, p. 256 ["The Mary-Child"]) it is said that the "Three-in-One" is in the forbidden room, which seems to me worth noting.
[44] Aelian (*De natura animalium*, I, 47) relates that Apollo condemned the ravens to perpetual thirst because a raven sent to fetch water dallied too long. In German folklore it is said that the raven has to suffer from thirst in June or August, the reason given being that he alone did not mourn at the death of Christ, and that he failed to return when Noah sent him forth from the ark. (Köhler, *Kleinere Schriften zur Märchenforschung*, p. 3.) For the raven as an allegory of evil, see the exhaustive account by Hugo Rahner, "Earth Spirit and Divine Spirit in Patristic Theology." On the other hand the raven is closely connected with Apollo

young man, moved by the virtue of compassion, slakes it, not with hyssop and gall, but with quickening water, whereupon the three nails fall out and the raven escapes through the open window. Thus the evil spirit regains his freedom, changes into the hunter, steals the princess for the second time, but this time locks her up in his hunting-lodge on earth. The secret scheme is partially unveiled: the princess must be brought down from the upper world to the world of men, which was evidently not possible without the help of the evil spirit and man's disobedience.

429   But since in the human world, too, the hunter of souls is the princess's master, the hero has to intervene anew, to which end, as we have seen, he filches the four-legged horse from the witch and breaks the three-legged spell of the magician. It was the triad that first transfixed the raven, and the triad also represents the power of the evil spirit. These are the two triads that point in opposite directions.

430   Turning now to quite another field, the realm of psychological experience, we know that three of the four functions of consciousness can become differentiated, i.e., conscious, while the other remains connected with the matrix, the unconscious, and is known as the "inferior" function. It is the Achilles heel of even the most heroic consciousness: somewhere the strong man is weak, the clever man foolish, the good man bad, and the reverse is also true. In our fairytale the triad appears as a mutilated quaternity. If only one leg could be added to the other three, it would make a whole. The enigmatic axiom of Maria runs: ". . . from the third comes the one as the fourth" (ἐκ τοῦ τρίτου τὸ ἓν τέταρτον)—which presumably means, when the third produces the fourth it at once produces unity. The lost component which is in the possession of the wolves belonging to the Great Mother is indeed only a quarter, but, together with the three, it makes a whole which does away with division and conflict.

---

as his sacred animal, and in the Bible too he has a positive significance. See Psalm 147 : 9: "He giveth to the beast his food, and to the young ravens which cry"; Job 38 : 41: "Who provideth for the raven his food? when his young ones cry unto God, they wander for lack of meat." Cf. also Luke 12 : 24. Ravens appear as true "ministering spirits" in I Kings 17 : 6, where they bring Elijah the Tishbite his daily fare.

431   But how is it that a quarter, on the evidence of symbolism, is at the same time a triad? Here the symbolism of our fairytale leaves us in the lurch, and we are obliged to have recourse to the facts of psychology. I have said previously that three functions can become differentiated, and only one remains under the spell of the unconscious. This statement must be defined more closely. It is an empirical fact that only *one* function becomes more or less successfully differentiated, which on that account is known as the superior or main function, and together with extraversion or introversion constitutes the type of conscious attitude. This function has associated with it one or two partially differentiated auxiliary functions which hardly ever attain the same degree of differentiation as the main function, that is, the same degree of applicability by the will. Accordingly they possess a higher degree of spontaneity than the main function, which displays a large measure of reliability and is amenable to our intentions. The fourth, inferior function proves on the other hand to be inaccessible to our will. It appears now as a teasing and distracting imp, now as a *deus ex machina*. But always it comes and goes of its own volition. From this it is clear that even the differentiated functions have only partially freed themselves from the unconscious; for the rest they are still rooted in it and to that extent they operate under its rule. Hence the three "differentiated" functions at the disposal of the ego have three corresponding unconscious components that have not yet broken loose from the unconscious.[45] And just as the three conscious and differentiated parts of these functions are confronted by a fourth, undifferentiated function which acts as a painfully disturbing factor, so also the superior function seems to have its worst enemy in the unconscious. Nor should we omit to mention one final turn of the screw: like the devil who delights in disguising himself as an angel of light, the inferior function secretly and mischievously influences the superior function most of all, just as the latter represses the former most strongly.[46]

432   These unfortunately somewhat abstract formulations are necessary in order to throw some light on the tricky and allusive

45 Pictured as three princesses, buried neck deep, in *Nordische Volksmärchen*, II, pp. 126ff. ["The Three Princesses in the White Land"].
46 For the function theory, see *Psychological Types*.

associations in our—save the mark!—"childishly simple" fairy-tale. The two antithetical triads, the one banning and the other representing the power of evil, tally to a hair's breadth with the functional structure of the conscious and unconscious psyche. Being a spontaneous, naïve, and uncontrived product of the psyche, the fairytale cannot very well express anything except what the psyche actually is. It is not only *our* fairytale that depicts these structural psychic relations, but countless other fairytales do the same.[47]

433   Our fairytale reveals with unusual clarity the essentially antithetical nature of the spirit archetype, while on the other hand it shows the bewildering play of antinomies all aiming at the great goal of higher consciousness. The young swineherd who climbs from the animal level up to the top of the giant world-tree and there, in the upper world of light, discovers his captive anima, the high-born princess, symbolizes the ascent of consciousness, rising from almost bestial regions to a lofty perch with a broad outlook, which is a singularly appropriate image for the enlargement of the conscious horizon.[48] Once the masculine consciousness has attained this height, it comes face to face with its feminine counterpart, the anima.[49] She is a personification of the unconscious. The meeting shows how inept it is to designate the latter as the "subconscious": it is not merely "below" consciousness but also above it, so far above it indeed that the hero has to climb up to it with considerable effort. This "upper" unconscious, however, is far from being a "superconscious" in the sense that anyone who reaches it, like our hero, would stand as high above the "subconscious" as above the earth's surface. On the contrary, he makes the disagreeable discovery that his high and mighty anima, the Princess Soul, is bewitched up there and no freer than a bird in a golden cage.

47 I would like to add, for the layman's benefit, that the theory of the psyche's structure was not derived from fairytales and myths, but is grounded on empirical observations made in the field of medico-psychological research and was corroborated only secondarily through the study of comparative symbology, in spheres very far removed from ordinary medical practice.

48 A typical enantiodromia is played out here: as one cannot go any higher along this road, one must now realize the other side of one's being, and climb down again.

49 The young man asks himself, on catching sight of the tree, "How would it be if you were to look at the world from the top of that great tree?"

He may pat himself on the back for having soared up from the flatlands and from almost bestial stupidity, but his soul is in the power of an evil spirit, a sinister father-imago of subterrene nature in the guise of a raven, the celebrated theriomorphic figure of the devil. What use now is his lofty perch and his wide horizon, when his own dear soul is languishing in prison? Worse, she plays the game of the underworld and ostensibly tries to stop the young man from discovering the secret of her imprisonment, by forbidding him to enter that one room. But secretly she leads him to it by the very fact of her veto. It is as though the unconscious had two hands of which one always does the opposite of the other. The princess wants and does not want to be rescued. But the evil spirit too has got himself into a fix, by all accounts: he wanted to filch a fine soul from the shining upper world—which he could easily do as a winged being—but had not bargained on being shut up there himself. Black spirit though he is, he longs for the light. That is his secret justification, just as his being spellbound is a punishment for his transgression. But so long as the evil spirit is caught in the upper world, the princess cannot get down to earth either, and the hero remains lost in paradise. So now he commits the sin of disobedience and thereby enables the robber to escape, thus causing the abduction of the princess for the second time—a whole chain of calamities. In the result, however, the princess comes down to earth and the devilish raven assumes the human shape of the hunter. The other-worldly anima and the evil principle both descend to the human sphere, that is, they dwindle to human proportions and thus become approachable. The three-legged, all-knowing horse represents the hunter's own power: it corresponds to the unconscious components of the differentiated functions.[50] The hunter himself personifies the inferior function, which also manifests itself in the hero as his inquisitiveness and love of adventure. As the story unfolds, he becomes more and more like the hunter: he too obtains his horse from the witch. But, unlike him, the hunter omitted to

---

[50] The "omniscience" of the unconscious components is naturally an exaggeration. Nevertheless they do have at their disposal—or are influenced by—subliminal perceptions and memories of the unconscious, as well as by its instinctive archetypal contents. It is these that give unconscious activities their unexpectedly accurate information.

obtain the twelve lambs in order to feed the wolves, who then injured his horse. He forgot to pay tribute to the chthonic powers because he was nothing but a robber. Through this omission the hero learns that the unconscious lets its creatures go only at the cost of sacrifice.[51] The number 12 is presumably a time symbol, with the subsidiary meaning of the twelve labours (ἄθλα) [52] that have to be performed for the unconscious before one can get free.[53] The hunter looks like a previous unsuccessful attempt of the hero to gain possession of his soul through robbery and violence. But the conquest of the soul is in reality a work of patience, self-sacrifice, and devotion. By gaining possession of the four-legged horse the hero steps right into the shoes of the hunter and carries off the princess as well. The quaternity in our tale proves to be the greater power, for it integrates into its totality that which it still needed in order to become whole.

434   The archetype of the spirit in this, be it said, by no means primitive fairytale is expressed theriomorphically as a system of three functions which is subordinated to a unity, the evil spirit, in the same way that some unnamed authority has crucified the raven with a triad of three nails. The two supraordinate unities correspond in the first case to the inferior function which is the arch-enemy of the main function, namely to the hunter; and in the second case to the main function, namely to the hero. Hunter and hero are ultimately equated with one another, so that the hunter's function is resolved in the hero. As a matter of fact, the hero lies dormant in the hunter from the very beginning, egging him on, with all the unmoral means at his disposal, to carry out the rape of the soul, and then causing him to play her into the hero's hands against the hunter's will. On the surface a furious conflict rages between them, but down below the one goes about the other's business. The knot is unravelled directly the hero succeeds in capturing the quaternity—or in psychological language, when he assimilates the inferior function

51 The hunter has reckoned without his host, as generally happens. Seldom or never do we think of the price exacted by the spirit's activity.
52 Cf. the Heracles cycle.
53 The alchemists stress the long duration of the work and speak of the "longissima via," "diuturnitas immensae meditationis," etc. The number 12 may be connected with the ecclesiastical year, in which the redemptive work of Christ is fulfilled. The lamb-sacrifice probably comes from this source too.

into the ternary system. That puts an end to the conflict at one blow, and the figure of the hunter melts into thin air. After this victory, the hero sets his princess upon the three-legged steed and together they ride away to her father's kingdom. From now on she rules and personifies the realm of spirit that formerly served the wicked hunter. Thus the anima is and remains the representative of that part of the unconscious which can never be assimilated into a humanly attainable whole.

435   *Postscript.* Only after the completion of my manuscript was my attention drawn by a friend to a Russian variant of our story. It bears the title "Maria Morevna." [54] The hero of the story is no swineherd, but Czarevitch Ivan. There is an interesting explanation of the three helpful animals: they correspond to Ivan's three sisters and their husbands, who are really birds. The three sisters represent an unconscious triad of functions related to both the animal and spiritual realms. The bird-men are a species of angel and emphasize the auxiliary nature of the unconscious functions. In the story they intervene at the critical moment when the hero—unlike his German counterpart—gets into the power of the evil spirit and is killed and dismembered (the typical fate of the God-man!).[55] The evil spirit is an old man who is often shown naked and is called Koschei [56] the Deathless. The corresponding witch is the well-known Baba Yaga. The three helpful animals of the German variant are doubled here, appearing first as the bird-men and then as the lion, the strange bird, and the bees. The princess is Queen Maria Morevna, a redoubtable martial leader—Mary the queen of heaven is lauded in the Russian Orthodox hymnal as "leader of hosts"!—who has chained up the evil spirit with twelve chains in the forbidden room in her castle. When Ivan slakes the old devil's thirst he makes off with the queen. The magic riding animals do not in the end turn into human beings. This Russian story has a distinctly more primitive character.

54 "Daughter of the sea."—Afanas'ev, *Russian Fairy Tales,* pp. 553ff.
55 The old man puts the dismembered body into a barrel which he throws into the sea. This is reminiscent of the fate of Osiris (head and phallus).
56 From *kost,* 'bone,' and *pakost, kapost,* 'disgusting, dirty.'

V. SUPPLEMENT

436   The following remarks lay no claim to general interest, being in the main technical. I wanted at first to delete them from this revised version of my essay, but then I changed my mind and appended them in a supplement. The reader who is not specifically interested in psychology can safely skip this section. For, in what follows, I have dealt with the abstruse-looking problem of the three- and four-leggedness of the magic horses, and presented my reflections in such a way as to demonstrate the method I have employed. This piece of psychological reasoning rests firstly on the irrational data of the material, that is, of the fairytale, myth, or dream, and secondly on the conscious realization of the "latent" rational connections which these data have with one another. That such connections exist at all is something of a hypothesis, like that which asserts that dreams have a meaning. The truth of this assumption is not established *a priori:* its usefulness can only be proved by application. It therefore remains to be seen whether its methodical application to irrational material enables one to interpret the latter in a meaningful way. Its application consists in approaching the material as if it had a coherent inner meaning. For this purpose most of the data require a certain amplification, that is, they need to be clarified, generalized, and approximated to a more or less general concept in accordance with Cardan's rule of interpretation. For instance, the three-leggedness, in order to be recognized for what it is, has first to be separated from the horse and then approximated to its specific principle—the principle of threeness. Likewise, the four-leggedness in the fairytale, when raised to the level of a general concept, enters into relationship with the threeness, and as a result we have the enigma mentioned in the *Timaeus,* the problem of three and four. Triads and tetrads represent archetypal structures that play a significant part in all symbolism and are equally important for the investigation of myths and dreams. By raising the irrational datum (three-leggedness and four-leggedness) to the level of a general concept we elicit the universal meaning of this motif and encourage the inquiring mind to tackle the problem seriously. This task involves a series of reflections and deductions of a

121

technical nature which I would not wish to withhold from the psychologically interested reader and especially from the professional, the less so as this labour of the intellect represents a typical unravelling of symbols and is indispensable for an adequate understanding of the products of the unconscious. Only in this way can the nexus of unconscious relationships be made to yield their own meaning, in contrast to those deductive interpretations derived from a preconceived theory, e.g., interpretations based on astronomy, meteorology, mythology, and—last but not least—the sexual theory.

437   The three-legged and four-legged horses are in truth a recondite matter worthy of closer examination. The three and the four remind us not only of the dilemma we have already met in the theory of psychological functions, but also of the axiom of Maria Prophetissa, which plays a considerable role in alchemy. It may therefore be rewarding to examine more closely the meaning of the miraculous horses.

438   The first thing that seems to me worthy of note is that the three-legged horse which is assigned to the princess as her mount is a mare, and is moreover herself a bewitched princess. Threeness is unmistakably connected here with femininity, whereas from the dominating religious standpoint of consciousness it is an exclusively masculine affair, quite apart from the fact that 3, as an uneven number, is masculine in the first place. One could therefore translate threeness as "masculinity" outright, this being all the more significant when one remembers the ancient Egyptian triunity of God, Ka-mutef,[57] and Pharaoh.

439   Three-leggedness, as the attribute of some animal, denotes the unconscious masculinity immanent in a female creature. In a real woman it would correspond to the animus who, like the magic horse, represents "spirit." In the case of the anima, however, threeness does not coincide with any Christian idea of the Trinity but with the "lower triangle," the inferior function triad that constitutes the "shadow." The inferior half of the personality is for the greater part unconscious. It does not denote the whole of the unconscious, but only the personal segment of it. The anima, on the other hand, so far as she is distinguished from the shadow, personifies the collective un-

[57] Ka-mutef means "bull of his mother." See Jacobsohn, "Die dogmatische Stellung des Königs in der Theologie der alten Aegypter," pp. 17, 35, 41ff.

conscious. If threeness is assigned to her as a riding-animal, it means that she "rides" the shadow, is related to it as the *mar*.[58] In that case she possesses the shadow. But if she herself is the horse, then she has lost her dominating position as a personification of the collective unconscious and is "ridden"—possessed —by Princess A, spouse of the hero. As the fairytale rightly says, she has been changed by witchcraft into the three-legged horse (Princess B).

We can sort out this imbroglio more or less as follows:

440   1. Princess A is the anima [59] of the hero. She rides—that is, possesses—the three-legged horse, who is the shadow, the inferior function-triad of her later spouse. To put it more simply: she has taken possession of the inferior half of the hero's personality. She has caught him on his weak side, as so often happens in ordinary life, for where one is weak one needs support and completion. In fact, a woman's place is on the weak side of a man. This is how we would have to formulate the situation if we regarded the hero and Princess A as two ordinary people. But since it is a fairy-story played out mainly in the world of magic, we are probably more correct in interpreting Princess A as the hero's anima. In that case the hero has been wafted out of the profane world through his encounter with the anima, like Merlin by his fairy: as an ordinary man he is like one caught in a marvellous dream, viewing the world through a veil of mist.

441   2. The matter is now considerably complicated by the unexpected fact that the three-legged horse is a mare, an equivalent of Princess A. She (the mare) is Princess B, who in the shape of a horse corresponds to Princess A's shadow (i.e., her inferior function-triad). Princess B, however, differs from Princess A in that, unlike her, she does not ride the horse but is contained in it: she is bewitched and has thus come under the spell of a masculine triad. Therefore, she is possessed by a shadow.

442   3. The question now is, *whose* shadow? It cannot be the shadow of the hero, for this is already taken up by the latter's

[58] Cf. *Symbols of Transformation,* pp. 249–51, 277.
[59] The fact that she is no ordinary girl, but is of royal descent and moreover the *electa* of the evil spirit, proves her nonhuman, mythological nature. I must assume that the reader is acquainted with the idea of the anima.

anima. The fairytale gives us the answer: it is the hunter or magician who has bewitched her. As we have seen, the hunter is somehow connected with the hero, since the latter gradually puts himself in his shoes. Hence one could easily arrive at the conjecture that the hunter is at bottom none other than the shadow of the hero. But this supposition is contradicted by the fact that the hunter stands for a formidable power which extends not only to the hero's anima but much further, namely to the royal brother-sister pair of whose existence the hero and his anima have no notion, and who appear very much out of the blue in the story itself. The power that extends beyond the orbit of the individual has a more than individual character and cannot therefore be identified with the shadow, if we conceive and define this as the dark half of the personality. As a supra-individual factor the numen of the hunter is a dominant of the collective unconscious, and its characteristic features— hunter, magician, raven, miraculous horse, crucifixion or suspension high up in the boughs of the world-tree [60]—touch the Germanic psyche very closely. Hence the Christian *Weltanschauung*, when reflected in the ocean of the (Germanic) unconscious, logically takes on the features of Wotan.[61] In the figure of the hunter we meet an *imago dei,* a God-image, for Wotan is also a god of winds and spirits, on which account the Romans fittingly interpreted him as Mercury.

443   4. The Prince and his sister, Princess B, have therefore been seized by a pagan god and changed into horses, i.e., thrust down to the animal level, into the realm of the unconscious. The inference is that in their proper human shape the pair of them

---

[60] "I ween that I hung / on the windy tree,
    Hung there for nights full nine;
    With the spear I was wounded, / and offered I was
    To Othin, myself to myself,
    On the tree that none / may ever know
    What root beneath it runs."
                    —*Hovamol,* 139 (trans. by H. A. Bellows, p. 60).
[61] Cf. the experience of God as described by Nietzsche in "Ariadne's Lament":
        "I am but thy quarry,
        Cruellest of hunters!
        Thy proudest captive,
        Thou brigand back of the clouds!"
                    —*Gedichte und Sprüche,* pp. 155ff.

once belonged to the sphere of collective consciousness. But who are they?

444   In order to answer this question we must proceed from the fact that these two are an undoubted counterpart of the hero and Princess A. They are connected with the latter also because they serve as their mounts, and in consequence they appear as their lower, animal halves. Because of its almost total unconsciousness, the animal has always symbolized the psychic sphere in man which lies hidden in the darkness of the body's instinctual life. The hero rides the stallion, characterized by the even (feminine) number 4; Princess A rides the mare who has only three legs (3 = a masculine number). These numbers make it clear that the transformation into animals has brought with it a modification of sex character: the stallion has a feminine attribute, the mare a masculine one. Psychology can confirm this development as follows: to the degree that a man is overpowered by the (collective) unconscious there is not only a more unbridled intrusion of the instinctual sphere, but a certain feminine character also makes its appearance, which I have suggested should be called "anima." If, on the other hand, a woman comes under the domination of the unconscious, the darker side of her feminine nature emerges all the more strongly, coupled with markedly masculine traits. These latter are comprised under the term "animus." [62]

445   5. According to the fairytale, however, the animal form of the brother-sister pair is "unreal" and due simply to the magic influence of the pagan hunter-god. If they were nothing but animals, we could rest content with this interpretation. But that would be to pass over in unmerited silence the singular allusion to a modification of sex character. The white horses are no ordinary horses: they are miraculous beasts with supernatural powers. Therefore the human figures out of which the horses were magically conjured must likewise have had something supernatural about them. The fairytale makes no comment here, but if our assumption is correct that the two animal forms correspond to the subhuman components of hero and princess, then it follows that the human forms—Prince and Princess B—must correspond to their superhuman components. The

[62] Cf. Emma Jung, "On the Nature of the Animus."

superhuman quality of the original swineherd is shown by the fact that he becomes a hero, practically a half-god, since he does not stay with his swine but climbs the world-tree, where he is very nearly made its prisoner, like Wotan. Similarly, he could not have become like the hunter if he did not have a certain resemblance to him in the first place. In the same way the imprisonment of Princess A on the top of the world-tree proves her electness, and in so far as she shares the hunter's bed, as stated by the tale, she is actually the bride of God.

446   It is these extraordinary forces of heroism and election, bordering on the superhuman, which involve two quite ordinary humans in a superhuman fate. Accordingly, in the profane world a swineherd becomes a king, and a princess gets an agreeable husband. But since, for fairytales, there is not only a profane but also a magical world, human fate does not have the final word. The fairytale therefore does not omit to point out what happens in the world of magic. There too a prince and princess have got into the power of the evil spirit, who is himself in a tight corner from which he cannot extricate himself without extraneous help. So the human fate that befalls the swineherd and Princess A is paralleled in the world of magic. But in so far as the hunter is a pagan God-image and thus exalted above the world of heroes and paramours of the gods, the parallelism goes beyond the merely magical into a divine and spiritual sphere, where the evil spirit, the Devil himself— or at least a devil—is bound by the spell of an equally mighty or even mightier counter-principle indicated by the three nails. This supreme tension of opposites, the mainspring of the whole drama, is obviously the conflict between the upper and lower triads, or, to put it in theological terms, between the Christian God and the devil who has assumed the features of Wotan.[63]

447   6. We must, it seems, start from this highest level if we want to understand the story correctly, for the drama takes its rise from the initial transgression of the evil spirit. The immediate consequence of this is his crucifixion. In that distressing situation he needs outside help, and as it is not forthcoming from above, it can only be summoned from below. A young swine-

[63] As regards the triadic nature of Wotan cf. Ninck, *Wodan und germanischer Schicksalsglaube*, p. 142. His horse is also described as, among other things, three-legged.

herd, possessed with the boyish spirit of adventure, is reckless and inquisitive enough to climb the world-tree. Had he fallen and broken his neck, no doubt everybody would have said, "What evil spirit could have given him the crazy idea of climbing up an enormous tree like that!" Nor would they have been altogether wrong, for that is precisely what the evil spirit was after. The capture of Princess A was a transgression in the profane world, and the bewitching of the—as we may suppose— semidivine brother-sister pair was just such an enormity in the magical world. We do not know, but it is possible, that this heinous crime was committed before the bewitching of Princess A. At any rate, both episodes point to a transgression of the evil spirit in the magical world as well as in the profane.

448   It is assuredly not without a deeper meaning that the rescuer or redeemer should be a swineherd, like the Prodigal Son. He is of lowly origin and has this much in common with the curious conception of the redeemer in alchemy. His first liberating act is to deliver the evil spirit from the divine punishment meted out to him. It is from this act, representing the first stage of the lysis, that the whole dramatic tangle develops.

449   7. The moral of this story is in truth exceedingly odd. The finale satisfies in so far as the swineherd and Princess A are married and become the royal pair. Prince and Princess B likewise celebrate their wedding, but this—in accordance with the archaic prerogative of kings—takes the form of incest, which, though somewhat repellent, must be regarded as more or less habitual in semidivine circles.[64] But what, we may ask, happens to the evil spirit, whose rescue from condign punishment sets the whole thing in motion? The wicked hunter is trampled to pieces by the horses, which presumably does no lasting damage to a spirit. Apparently he vanishes without trace, but only apparently, for he does after all leave a trace behind him, namely a hard-won happiness in both the profane and the magical world. Two halves of the quaternity, represented on one side by the swineherd and Princess A and on the other by

---

[64] The assumption that they are a brother-sister pair is supported by the fact that the stallion addresses the mare as "sister." This may be just a figure of speech; on the other hand sister means sister, whether we take it figuratively or non-figuratively. Moreover, incest plays a significant part in mythology as well as in alchemy.

Prince and Princess B, have each come together and united: two marriage-pairs now confront one another, parallel but otherwise divided, inasmuch as the one pair belongs to the profane and the other to the magical world. But in spite of this indubitable division, secret psychological connections, as we have seen, exist between them which allow us to derive the one pair from the other.

450   Speaking in the spirit of the fairytale, which unfolds its drama from the highest point, one would have to say that the world of half-gods is anterior to the profane world and produces it out of itself, just as the world of half-gods must be thought of as proceeding from the world of gods. Conceived in this way, the swineherd and Princess A are nothing less than earthly simulacra of Prince and Princess B, who in their turn would be the descendants of divine prototypes. Nor should we forget that the horse-breeding witch belongs to the hunter as his female counterpart, rather like an ancient Epona (the Celtic goddess of horses). Unfortunately we are not told how the magical conjuration into horses happened. But it is evident that the witch had a hand in the game because both the horses were raised from her stock and are thus, in a sense, her productions. Hunter and witch form a pair—the reflection, in the nocturnal-chthonic part of the magical world, of a divine parental pair. The latter is easily recognized in the central Christian idea of *sponsus et sponsa,* Christ and his bride, the Church.

451   If we wanted to explain the fairytale personalistically, the attempt would founder on the fact that archetypes are not whimsical inventions but autonomous elements of the unconscious psyche which were there before any invention was thought of. They represent the unalterable structure of a psychic world whose "reality" is attested by the determining effects it has upon the conscious mind. Thus, it is a significant psychic reality that the human pair [65] is matched by another pair in the unconscious, the latter pair being only in appearance a reflection of the first. In reality the royal pair invariably comes first, as an *a priori,* so that the human pair has far more the significance of an individual concretization, in space and time, of

[65] Human in so far as the anima is replaced by a human person.

an eternal and primordial image—at least in its mental structure, which is imprinted upon the biological continuum.

452 We could say, then, that the swineherd stands for the "animal" man who has a soul-mate somewhere in the upper world. By her royal birth she betrays her connection with the pre-existent, semidivine pair. Looked at from this angle, the latter stands for everything a man can become if only he climbs high enough up the world-tree.[66] For to the degree that the young swineherd gains possession of the patrician, feminine half of himself, he approximates to the pair of half-gods and lifts himself into the sphere of royalty, which means universal validity. We come across the same theme in Christian Rosencreutz's *Chymical Wedding*, where the king's son must first free his bride from the power of a Moor, to whom she has voluntarily given herself as a concubine. The Moor represents the alchemical *nigredo* in which the arcane substance lies hidden, an idea that forms yet another parallel to our mythologem, or, as we would say in psychological language, another variant of this archetype.

453 As in alchemy, our fairytale describes the unconscious processes that compensate the conscious, Christian situation. It depicts the workings of a spirit who carries our Christian thinking beyond the boundaries set by ecclesiastical concepts, seeking an answer to questions which neither the Middle Ages nor the present day have been able to solve. It is not difficult to see in the image of the second royal pair a correspondence to the ecclesiastical conception of bridegroom and bride, and in that of the hunter and witch a distortion of it, veering towards an atavistic, unconscious Wotanism. The fact that it is a *German* fairytale makes the position particularly interesting, since this same Wotanism was the psychological godfather of National Socialism, a phenomenon which carried the distortion to the lowest pitch before the eyes of the world.[67] On the other hand, the fairytale makes it clear that it is possible for a man to attain totality, to become whole, only with the co-operation of the spirit of darkness, indeed that the latter is actually a *causa*

[66] The great tree corresponds to the *arbor philosophica* of the alchemists. The meeting between an earthly human being and the anima, swimming down in the shape of a mermaid, is to be found in the so-called "Ripley Scrowle." Cf. *Psychology and Alchemy*, fig. 257.   [67] Cf. my "Wotan."

instrumentalis of redemption and individuation. In utter perversion of this goal of spiritual development, to which all nature aspires and which is also prefigured in Christian doctrine, National Socialism destroyed man's moral autonomy and set up the nonsensical totalitarianism of the State. The fairytale tells us how to proceed if we want to overcome the power of darkness: we must turn his own weapons against him, which naturally cannot be done if the magical underworld of the hunter remains unconscious, and if the best men in the nation would rather preach dogmatisms and platitudes than take the human psyche seriously.

VI. CONCLUSION

454   When we consider the spirit in its archetypal form as it appears to us in fairytales and dreams, it presents a picture that differs strangely from the conscious idea of spirit, which is split up into so many meanings. Spirit was originally a spirit in human or animal form, a *daimonion* that came upon man from without. But our material already shows traces of an expansion of consciousness which has gradually begun to occupy that originally unconscious territory and to transform those *daimonia,* at least partially, into voluntary acts. Man conquers not only nature, but spirit also, without realizing what he is doing. To the man of enlightened intellect it seems like the correction of a fallacy when he recognizes that what he took to be spirits is simply the human spirit and ultimately his own spirit. All the superhuman things, whether good or bad, that former ages predicated of the *daimonia,* are reduced to "reasonable" proportions as though they were pure exaggeration, and everything seems to be in the best possible order. But were the unanimous convictions of the past really and truly only exaggerations? If they were not, then the integration of the spirit means nothing less than its demonization, since the superhuman spiritual agencies that were formerly tied up in nature are introjected into human nature, thus endowing it with a power which extends the bounds of the personality *ad infinitum,* in the most perilous way. I put it to the enlightened rationalist: has his rational

reduction led to the beneficial control of matter and spirit? He will point proudly to the advances in physics and medicine, to the freeing of the mind from medieval stupidity and—as a well-meaning Christian—to our deliverance from the fear of demons. But we continue to ask: what have all our other cultural achievements led to? The fearful answer is there before our eyes: man has been delivered from no fear, a hideous nightmare lies upon the world. So far reason has failed lamentably, and the very thing that everybody wanted to avoid rolls on in ghastly progression. Man has achieved a wealth of useful gadgets, but, to offset that, he has torn open the abyss, and what will become of him now—where can he make a halt? After the last World War we hoped for reason: we go on hoping. But already we are fascinated by the possibilities of atomic fission and promise ourselves a Golden Age—the surest guarantee that the abomination of desolation will grow to limitless dimensions. And who or what is it that causes all this? It is none other than that harmless (!), ingenious, inventive, and sweetly reasonable human spirit who unfortunately is abysmally unconscious of the demonism that still clings to him. Worse, this spirit does everything to avoid looking himself in the face, and we all help him like mad. Only, heaven preserve us from psychology—*that* depravity might lead to self-knowledge! Rather let us have wars, for which somebody else is always to blame, nobody seeing that all the world is driven to do just what all the world flees from in terror.

455　　It seems to me, frankly, that former ages did not exaggerate, that the spirit has not sloughed off its demonisms, and that mankind, because of its scientific and technological development, has in increasing measure delivered itself over to the danger of possession. True, the archetype of the spirit is capable of working for good as well as for evil, but it depends upon man's free—i.e., conscious—decision whether the good also will be perverted into something satanic. Man's worst sin is unconsciousness, but it is indulged in with the greatest piety even by those who should serve mankind as teachers and examples. When shall we stop taking man for granted in this barbarous manner and in all seriousness seek ways and means to exorcize him, to rescue him from possession and unconsciousness, and make this the most vital task of civilization? Can we not understand that all the outward tinkerings and improvements do not touch man's inner nature, and that everything ultimately depends upon whether the man who wields the science and the technics is capable of responsibility or not? Christianity has shown us the way, but, as the facts bear witness, it has not penetrated deeply enough below the surface. What depths of despair are still needed to open the eyes of the world's responsible leaders, so that at least they can refrain from leading themselves into temptation?

IV

ON THE PSYCHOLOGY
OF THE TRICKSTER-FIGURE

ON THE PSYCHOLOGY OF THE
TRICKSTER-FIGURE [1]

456   It is no light task for me to write about the figure of the trickster in American Indian mythology within the confined space of a commentary. When I first came across Adolf Bandelier's classic on this subject, *The Delight Makers,* many years ago, I was struck by the European analogy of the carnival in the medieval Church, with its reversal of the hierarchic order, which is still continued in the carnivals held by student societies today. Something of this contradictoriness also inheres in the medieval description of the devil as *simia dei* (the ape of God), and in his characterization in folklore as the "simpleton" who is "fooled" or "cheated." A curious combination of typical trickster motifs can be found in the alchemical figure of Mercurius; for instance, his fondness for sly jokes and malicious pranks, his powers as a shape-shifter, his dual nature, half animal, half divine, his exposure to all kinds of tortures, and—last but not least—his approximation to the figure of a saviour. These qualities make Mercurius seem like a daemonic being resurrected from primitive times, older even than the Greek Hermes. His rogueries relate him in some measure to various figures met with in folklore and universally known in fairytales: Tom Thumb, Stupid Hans, or the buffoon-like Hanswurst, who is an altogether negative hero and yet manages to achieve through his stupidity what others fail to accomplish with their best efforts. In Grimm's fairytale, the "Spirit Mercurius" lets himself be outwitted by a peasant lad, and then has to buy his freedom with the precious gift of healing.

1 [Originally published as part 5 of *Der göttliche Schelm,* by Paul Radin, with commentaries by C. G. Jung and Karl Kerényi (Zurich, 1954). The present translation then appeared in the English version of the volume: *The Trickster: A Study in American Indian Mythology* (London and New York, 1956); it is republished here with only minor revisions.—EDITORS.]

457   Since all mythical figures correspond to inner psychic experiences and originally sprang from them, it is not surprising to find certain phenomena in the field of parapsychology which remind us of the trickster. These are the phenomena connected with poltergeists, and they occur at all times and places in the ambience of pre-adolescent children. The malicious tricks played by the poltergeist are as well known as the low level of his intelligence and the fatuity of his "communications." Ability to change his shape seems also to be one of his characteristics, as there are not a few reports of his appearance in animal form. Since he has on occasion described himself as a soul in hell, the motif of subjective suffering would seem not to be lacking either. His universality is co-extensive, so to speak, with that of shamanism, to which, as we know, the whole phenomenology of spiritualism belongs. There is something of the trickster in the character of the shaman and medicine-man, for he, too, often plays malicious jokes on people, only to fall victim in his turn to the vengeance of those whom he has injured. For this reason, his profession sometimes puts him in peril of his life. Besides that, the shamanistic techniques in themselves often cause the medicine-man a good deal of discomfort, if not actual pain. At all events the "making of a medicine-man" involves, in many parts of the world, so much agony of body and soul that permanent psychic injuries may result. His "approximation to the saviour" is an obvious consequence of this, in confirmation of the mythological truth that the wounded wounder is the agent of healing, and that the sufferer takes away suffering.

458   These mythological features extend even to the highest regions of man's spiritual development. If we consider, for example, the daemonic features exhibited by Yahweh in the Old Testament, we shall find in them not a few reminders of the unpredictable behaviour of the trickster, of his senseless orgies of destruction and his self-imposed sufferings, together with the same gradual development into a saviour and his simultaneous humanization. It is just this transformation of the meaningless into the meaningful that reveals the trickster's compensatory relation to the "saint." In the early Middle Ages, this led to some strange ecclesiastical customs based on memories of the ancient saturnalia. Mostly they were celebrated on the days immediately following the birth of Christ—that is, in

the New Year—with singing and dancing. The dances were the originally harmless *tripudia* of the priests, lower clergy, children, and subdeacons and took place in church. An *episcopus puerorum* (children's bishop) was elected on Innocents' Day and dressed in pontifical robes. Amid uproarious rejoicings he paid an official visit to the palace of the archbishop and bestowed the episcopal blessing from one of the windows. The same thing happened at the *tripudium hypodiaconorum,* and at the dances for other priestly grades. By the end of the twelfth century, the subdeacons' dance had degenerated into a real *festum stultorum* (fools' feast). A report from the year 1198 says that at the Feast of the Circumcision in Notre Dame, Paris, "so many abominations and shameful deeds" were committed that the holy place was desecrated "not only by smutty jokes, but even by the shedding of blood." In vain did Pope Innocent III inveigh against the "jests and madness that make the clergy a mockery," and the "shameless frenzy of their play-acting." Two hundred and fifty years later (March 12, 1444), a letter from the Theological Faculty of Paris to all the French bishops was still fulminating against these festivals, at which "even the priests and clerics elected an archbishop or a bishop or pope, and named him the Fools' Pope" *(fatuorum papam).* "In the very midst of divine service masqueraders with grotesque faces, disguised as women, lions, and mummers, performed their dances, sang indecent songs in the choir, ate their greasy food from a corner of the altar near the priest celebrating mass, got out their games of dice, burned a stinking incense made of old shoe leather, and ran and hopped about all over the church." [2]

459   It is not surprising that this veritable witches' sabbath was uncommonly popular, and that it required considerable time and effort to free the Church from this pagan heritage.[3]

---

[2] Du Cange, *Glossarium,* s.v. Kalendae, p. 1666. Here there is a note to the effect that the French title "sou-diacres" means literally 'saturi diaconi' or 'diacres saouls' (drunken deacons).

[3] These customs seem to be directly modelled on the pagan feast known as "Cervula" or "Cervulus." It took place on the kalends of January and was a kind of New Year's festival, at which people exchanged *strenae* (étrennes, 'gifts'), dressed up as animals or old women, and danced through the streets singing, to the applause of the populace. According to Du Cange (s.v. cervulus), sacrilegious songs were sung. This happened even in the immediate vicinity of St. Peter's in Rome.

460   In certain localities even the priests seem to have adhered to
the "libertas decembrica," as the Fools' Holiday was called, in
spite (or perhaps because?) of the fact that the older level of
consciousness could let itself rip on this happy occasion with all
the wildness, wantonness, and irresponsibility of paganism.[4]
These ceremonies, which still reveal the spirit of the trickster in
his original form, seem to have died out by the beginning of the
sixteenth century. At any rate, the various conciliar decrees
issued from 1581 to 1585 forbade only the *festum puerorum*
and the election of an *episcopus puerorum*.

461   Finally, we must also mention in this connection the *festum
asinorum*, which, so far as I know, was celebrated mainly in
France. Although considered a harmless festival in memory of
Mary's flight into Egypt, it was celebrated in a somewhat curious
manner which might easily have given rise to misunderstand-
ings. In Beauvais, the ass procession went right into the church.[5]
At the conclusion of each part (Introit, Kyrie, Gloria, etc.) of
the high mass that followed, the whole congregation *brayed*,
that is, they all went "Y-a" like a donkey ("hac modulatione
hinham concludebantur"). A codex dating apparently from the
eleventh century says: "At the end of the mass, instead of the
words 'Ite missa est,' the priest shall bray three times (*ter hin-
hamabit*), and instead of the words 'Deo gratias,' the congregation shall answer 'Y-a' (*hinham*) three times."

462   Du Cange cites a hymn from this festival:

> Orientis partibus
> Adventavit Asinus
> Pulcher et fortissimus
> Sarcinis aptissimus.

Each verse was followed by the French refrain:

[4] Part of the *festum fatuorum* in many places was the still unexplained ball-
game played by the priests and captained by the bishop or archbishop, "ut etiam
sese ad lusum pilae demittent" (that they also may indulge in the game of pelota).
Pila or *pelota* is the ball which the players throw to one another. See Du Cange,
s.v. Kalendae and pelota.
[5] "Puella, quae cum asino a parte Evangelii prope altare collocabatur" (the girl
who stationed herself with the ass at the side of the altar where the gospel is
read). Du Cange, s.v. festum asinorum.

> Hez, Sire Asnes, car chantez
> Belle bouche rechignez
> Vous aurez du foin assez
> Et de l'avoine à plantez.

The hymn had nine verses, the last of which was:

> Amen, dicas, Asine (*hic genuflectebatur*)
> Jam satur de gramine.
> Amen, amen, itera
> Aspernare vetera.[6]

4⁶³   Du Cange says that the more ridiculous this rite seemed, the greater the enthusiasm with which it was celebrated. In other places the ass was decked with a golden canopy whose corners were held "by distinguished canons"; the others present had to "don suitably festive garments, as at Christmas." Since there were certain tendencies to bring the ass into symbolic relationship with Christ, and since, from ancient times, the god of the Jews was vulgarly conceived to be an ass—a prejudice which extended to Christ himself,[7] as is shown by the mock crucifixion scratched on the wall of the Imperial Cadet School on the Palatine [8]—the danger of theriomorphism lay uncomfortably close. Even the bishops could do nothing to stamp out this custom, until finally it had to be suppressed by the "auctoritas supremi Senatus." The suspicion of blasphemy becomes quite

---

[6] *Caetera* instead of *vetera*? [Trans. by A. S. B. Glover:

> From the furthest Eastern clime
> Came the Ass in olden time,
> Comely, sturdy for the road,
> Fit to bear a heavy load.

> Sing then loudly, master Ass,
> Let the tempting titbit pass:
> You shall have no lack of hay
> And of oats find good supply.

> Say Amen, Amen, good ass, (*here a
>   genuflection is made*)
> Now you've had your fill of grass;
> Ancient paths are left behind:
> Sing Amen with gladsome mind.]

[7] Cf. also Tertullian, *Apologeticus adversus gentes*, XVI.

[8] [Reproduced in *Symbols of Transformation*, pl. XLIII.—EDITORS.]

open in Nietzsche's "Ass Festival," which is a deliberately blasphemous parody of the mass.[9]

464　　These medieval customs demonstrate the role of the trickster to perfection, and, when they vanished from the precincts of the Church, they appeared again on the profane level of Italian theatricals, as those comic types who, often adorned with enormous ithyphallic emblems, entertained the far from prudish public with ribaldries in true Rabelaisian style. Callot's engravings have preserved these classical figures for posterity—the Pulcinellas, Cucorognas, Chico Sgarras, and the like.[10]

465　　In picaresque tales, in carnivals and revels, in magic rites of healing, in man's religious fears and exaltations, this phantom of the trickster haunts the mythology of all ages, sometimes in quite unmistakable form, sometimes in strangely modulated guise.[11] He is obviously a "psychologem," an archetypal psychic structure of extreme antiquity. In his clearest manifestations he is a faithful reflection of an absolutely undifferentiated human consciousness, corresponding to a psyche that has hardly left the animal level. That this is how the trickster figure originated can hardly be contested if we look at it from the causal and historical angle. In psychology as in biology we cannot afford to overlook or underestimate this question of origins, although the answer usually tells us nothing about the functional meaning. For this reason biology should never forget the question of purpose, for only by answering that can we get at the meaning of a phenomenon. Even in pathology, where we are concerned with lesions which have no meaning in themselves, the exclusively causal approach proves to be inadequate, since there are a number of pathological phenomena which only give up their meaning when we inquire into their purpose. And where we are concerned with the normal phenomena of life, this question of purpose takes undisputed precedence.

9 *Thus Spake Zarathustra*, Part. IV, ch. LXXVIII.

10 I am thinking here of the series called "Balli di Sfessania." The name is probably a reference to the Etrurian town of Fescennia, which was famous for its lewd songs. Hence "Fescennina licentia" in Horace, Fescenninus being the equivalent of φαλλικός.

11 Cf. the article "Daily Paper Pantheon," by A. McGlashan, in *The Lancet* (1953), p. 238, pointing out that the figures in comic-strips have remarkable archetypal analogies.

466   When, therefore, a primitive or barbarous consciousness forms a picture of itself on a much earlier level of development and continues to do so for hundreds or even thousands of years, undeterred by the contamination of its archaic qualities with differentiated, highly developed mental products, then the causal explanation is that the older the archaic qualities are, the more conservative and pertinacious is their behaviour. One simply cannot shake off the memory-image of things as they were, and drags it along like a senseless appendage.

467   This explanation, which is facile enough to satisfy the rationalistic requirements of our age, would certainly not meet with the approval of the Winnebagos, the nearest possessors of the trickster cycle. For them the myth is not in any sense a remnant—it is far too amusing for that, and an object of undivided enjoyment. For them it still "functions," provided that they have not been spoiled by civilization. For them there is no earthly reason to theorize about the meaning and purpose of myths, just as the Christmas-tree seems no problem at all to the naïve European. For the thoughtful observer, however, both trickster and Christmas-tree afford reason enough for reflection. Naturally it depends very much on the mentality of the observer what he thinks about these things. Considering the crude primitivity of the trickster cycle, it would not be surprising if one saw in this myth simply the reflection of an earlier, rudimentary stage of consciousness, which is what the trickster obviously seems to be.[12]

468   The only question that would need answering is whether such personified reflections exist at all in empirical psychology. As a matter of fact they do, and these experiences of split or double personality actually form the core of the earliest psychopathological investigations. The peculiar thing about these dissociations is that the split-off personality is not just a random one, but stands in a complementary or compensatory relationship to the ego-personality. It is a personification of traits of

---

12 Earlier stages of consciousness seem to leave perceptible traces behind them. For instance, the chakras of the Tantric system correspond by and large to the regions where consciousness was earlier localized, *anahata* corresponding to the breast region, *manipura* to the abdominal region, *svadhistana* to the bladder region, and *visuddha* to the larynx and the speech-consciousness of modern man. Cf. Avalon, *The Serpent Power*.

character which are sometimes worse and sometimes better than those the ego-personality possesses. A collective personification like the trickster is the product of an aggregate of individuals and is welcomed by each individual as something known to him, which would not be the case if it were just an individual out-growth.

469   Now if the myth were nothing but an historical remnant, one would have to ask why it has not long since vanished into the great rubbish-heap of the past, and why it continues to make its influence felt on the highest levels of civilization, even where, on account of his stupidity and grotesque scurrility, the trickster no longer plays the role of a "delight-maker." In many cultures his figure seems like an old river-bed in which the water still flows. One can see this best of all from the fact that the trickster motif does not crop up only in its mythical form but appears just as naïvely and authentically in the unsuspecting modern man—whenever, in fact, he feels himself at the mercy of annoying "accidents" which thwart his will and his actions with apparently malicious intent. He then speaks of "hoodoos" and "jinxes" or of the "mischievousness of the object." Here the trickster is represented by counter-tendencies in the unconscious, and in certain cases by a sort of second personality, of a puerile and inferior character, not unlike the personalities who announce themselves at spiritualistic séances and cause all those ineffably childish phenomena so typical of poltergeists. I have, I think, found a suitable designation for this character-component when I called it the *shadow*.[13] On the civilized level, it is regarded as a personal "gaffe," "slip," "faux pas," etc., which are then chalked up as defects of the conscious personality. We are no longer aware that in carnival customs and the like there are remnants of a collective shadow figure which prove that the personal shadow is in part descended from a numinous collective figure. This collective figure gradually breaks up under the impact of civilization, leaving traces in folklore which are difficult to recognize. But the main part of him gets personalized and is made an object of personal responsibility.

470   Radin's trickster cycle preserves the shadow in its pristine mythological form, and thus points back to a very much earlier

13 The same idea can be found in the Church Father Irenaeus, who calls it the "umbra." *Adversus haereses,* I, ii, 1.

stage of consciousness which existed before the birth of the myth, when the Indian was still groping about in a similar mental darkness. Only when his consciousness reached a higher level could he detach the earlier state from himself and objectify it, that is, say anything about it. So long as his consciousness was itself trickster-like, such a confrontation could obviously not take place. It was possible only when the attainment of a newer and higher level of consciousness enabled him to look back on a lower and inferior state. It was only to be expected that a good deal of mockery and contempt should mingle with this retrospect, thus casting an even thicker pall over man's memories of the past, which were pretty unedifying anyway. This phenomenon must have repeated itself innumerable times in the history of his mental development. The sovereign contempt with which our modern age looks back on the taste and intelligence of earlier centuries is a classic example of this, and there is an unmistakable allusion to the same phenomenon in the New Testament, where we are told in Acts 17:30 that God looked down from above (ὑπεριδών, *despiciens*) on the χρόνοι τῆς ἀγνοίας, the times of ignorance (or unconsciousness).

471   This attitude contrasts strangely with the still commoner and more striking idealization of the past, which is praised not merely as the "good old days" but as the Golden Age—and not just by uneducated and superstitious people, but by all those legions of theosophical enthusiasts who resolutely believe in the former existence and lofty civilization of Atlantis.

472   Anyone who belongs to a sphere of culture that seeks the perfect state somewhere in the past must feel very queerly indeed when confronted by the figure of the trickster. He is a forerunner of the saviour, and, like him, God, man, and animal at once. He is both subhuman and superhuman, a bestial and divine being, whose chief and most alarming characteristic is his unconsciousness. Because of it he is deserted by his (evidently human) companions, which seems to indicate that he has fallen below their level of consciousness. He is so unconscious of himself that his body is not a unity, and his two hands fight each other. He takes his anus off and entrusts it with a special task. Even his sex is optional despite its phallic qualities: he can turn himself into a woman and bear children. From his penis he makes all kinds of useful plants. This is a reference to

his original nature as a Creator, for the world is made from the body of a god.

473   On the other hand he is in many respects stupider than the animals, and gets into one ridiculous scrape after another. Although he is not really evil, he does the most atrocious things from sheer unconsciousness and unrelatedness. His imprisonment in animal unconsciousness is suggested by the episode where he gets his head caught inside the skull of an elk, and the next episode shows how he overcomes this condition by imprisoning the head of a hawk inside his own rectum. True, he sinks back into the former condition immediately afterwards, by falling under the ice, and is outwitted time after time by the animals, but in the end he succeeds in tricking the cunning coyote, and this brings back to him his saviour nature. The trickster is a primitive "cosmic" being of *divine-animal* nature, on the one hand superior to man because of his superhuman qualities, and on the other hand inferior to him because of his unreason and unconsciousness. He is no match for the animals either, because of his extraordinary clumsiness and lack of instinct. These defects are the marks of his *human* nature, which is not so well adapted to the environment as the animal's but, instead, has prospects of a much higher development of consciousness based on a considerable eagerness to learn, as is duly emphasized in the myth.

474   What the repeated telling of the myth signifies is the therapeutic anamnesis of contents which, for reasons still to be discussed, should never be forgotten for long. If they were nothing but the remnants of an inferior state it would be understandable if man turned his attention away from them, feeling that their reappearance was a nuisance. This is evidently by no means the case, since the trickster has been a source of amusement right down to civilized times, where he can still be recognized in the carnival figures of Pulcinella and the clown. That is one important reason for his still continuing to function. But it is not the only one, and certainly not the reason why this reflection of an extremely primitive state of consciousness solidified into a mythological personage. Mere vestiges of an early state that is dying out usually lose their energy at an increasing rate, otherwise they would never disappear. The last thing we would expect is that they would have the strength to solidify into a

mythological figure with its own cycle of legends—unless, of course, they received energy from outside, in this case from a higher level of consciousness or from sources in the unconscious which are not yet exhausted. To take a legitimate parallel from the psychology of the individual, namely the appearance of an impressive shadow figure antagonistically confronting a personal consciousness: this figure does not appear merely because it *still* exists in the individual, but because it rests on a dynamism whose existence can only be explained in terms of his actual situation, for instance because the shadow is so disagreeable to his ego-consciousness that it has to be repressed into the unconscious. This explanation does not quite meet the case here, because the trickster obviously represents a vanishing level of consciousness which increasingly lacks the power to take express and assert itself. Furthermore, repression would prevent it from vanishing, because repressed contents are the very ones that have the best chance of survival, as we know from experience that nothing is corrected in the unconscious. Lastly, the story of the trickster is not in the least disagreeable to the Winnebago consciousness or incompatible with it but, on the contrary, pleasurable and therefore not conducive to repression. It looks, therefore, as if the myth were actively sustained and fostered by consciousness. This may well be so, since that is the best and most successful method of keeping the shadow figure conscious and subjecting it to conscious criticism. Although, to begin with, this criticism has more the character of a positive evaluation, we may expect that with the progressive development of consciousness the cruder aspects of the myth will gradually fall away, even if the danger of its rapid disappearance under the stress of white civilization did not exist. We have often seen how certain customs, originally cruel or obscene, became mere vestiges in the course of time.[14]

475   The process of rendering this motif harmless takes an extremely long time, as its history shows; one can still detect traces of it even at a high level of civilization. Its longevity could also be explained by the strength and vitality of the state of consciousness described in the myth, and by the secret attrac-

---

[14] For instance, the ducking of the "Ueli" (from Udalricus = Ulrich, yokel, oaf, fool) in Basel during the second half of January was, if I remember correctly, forbidden by the police in the 1860's, after one of the victims died of pneumonia.

tion and fascination this has for the conscious mind. Although purely causal hypotheses in the biological sphere are not as a rule very satisfactory, due weight must nevertheless be given to the fact that in the case of the trickster a higher level of consciousness has covered up a lower one, and that the latter was already in retreat. His recollection, however, is mainly due to the interest which the conscious mind brings to bear on him, the inevitable concomitant being, as we have seen, the gradual civilizing, i.e., assimilation, of a primitive daemonic figure who was originally autonomous and even capable of causing possession.

476   To supplement the causal approach by a final one therefore enables us to arrive at more meaningful interpretations not only in medical psychology, where we are concerned with individual fantasies originating in the unconscious, but also in the case of collective fantasies, that is myths and fairytales.

477   As Radin points out, the civilizing process begins within the framework of the trickster cycle itself, and this is a clear indication that the original state has been overcome. At any rate the marks of deepest unconsciousness fall away from him; instead of acting in a brutal, savage, stupid, and senseless fashion, the trickster's behaviour towards the end of the cycle becomes quite useful and sensible. The devaluation of his earlier unconsciousness is apparent even in the myth, and one wonders what has happened to his evil qualities. The naïve reader may imagine that when the dark aspects disappear they are no longer there in reality. But that is not the case at all, as experience shows. What actually happens is that the conscious mind is then able to free itself from the fascination of evil and is no longer obliged to live it compulsively. The darkness and the evil have not gone up in smoke, they have merely withdrawn into the unconscious owing to loss of energy, where they remain unconscious so long as all is well with the conscious. But if the conscious should find itself in a critical or doubtful situation, then it soon becomes apparent that the shadow has not dissolved into nothing but is only waiting for a favourable opportunity to reappear as a projection upon one's neighbour. If this trick is successful, there is immediately created between them that world of primordial darkness where everything that is characteristic of the trickster can happen—even on the highest plane of

civilization. The best examples of these "monkey tricks," as popular speech aptly and truthfully sums up this state of affairs in which everything goes wrong and nothing intelligent happens except by mistake at the last moment, are naturally to be found in politics.

478   The so-called civilized man has forgotten the trickster. He remembers him only figuratively and metaphorically, when, irritated by his own ineptitude, he speaks of fate playing tricks on him or of things being bewitched. He never suspects that his own hidden and apparently harmless shadow has qualities whose dangerousness exceeds his wildest dreams. As soon as people get together in masses and submerge the individual, the shadow is mobilized, and, as history shows, may even be personified and incarnated.

479   The disastrous idea that everything comes to the human psyche from outside and that it is born a *tabula rasa* is responsible for the erroneous belief that under normal circumstances the individual is in perfect order. He then looks to the State for salvation, and makes society pay for his inefficiency. He thinks the meaning of existence would be discovered if food and clothing were delivered to him gratis on his own doorstep, or if everybody possessed an automobile. Such are the puerilities that rise up in place of an unconscious shadow and keep it unconscious. As a result of these prejudices, the individual feels totally dependent on his environment and loses all capacity for introspection. In this way his code of ethics is replaced by a knowledge of what is permitted or forbidden or ordered. How, under these circumstances, can one expect a soldier to subject an order received from a superior to ethical scrutiny? He has not yet made the discovery that he might be capable of spontaneous ethical impulses, and of performing them—even when no one is looking.

480   From this point of view we can see why the myth of the trickster was preserved and developed: like many other myths, it was supposed to have a therapeutic effect. It holds the earlier low intellectual and moral level before the eyes of the more highly developed individual, so that he shall not forget how things looked yesterday. We like to imagine that something which we do not understand does not help us in any way. But that is not always so. Seldom does a man understand with his

head alone, least of all when he is a primitive. Because of its numinosity the myth has a direct effect on the unconscious, no matter whether it is understood or not. The fact that its re-peated telling has not long since become obsolete can, I believe, be explained by its usefulness. The explanation is rather diffi-cult because two contrary tendencies are at work: the desire on the one hand to get out of the earlier condition and on the other hand not to forget it.[15] Apparently Radin has also felt this difficulty, for he says: "Viewed psychologically, it might be con-tended that the history of civilization is largely the account of the attempts of man to forget his transformation from an ani-mal into a human being." [16] A few pages further on he says (with reference to the Golden Age): "So stubborn a refusal to forget is not an accident." [17] And it is also no accident that we are forced to contradict ourselves as soon as we try to formulate man's paradoxical attitude to myth. Even the most enlightened of us will set up a Christmas-tree for his children without having the least idea what this custom means, and is invariably disposed to nip any attempt at interpretation in the bud. It is really aston-ishing to see how many so-called superstitions are rampant nowadays in town and country alike, but if one took hold of the individual and asked him, loudly and clearly, "Do you be-lieve in ghosts? in witches? in spells and magic?" he would deny it indignantly. It is a hundred to one he has never heard of such things and thinks it all rubbish. But in secret he is all for it, just like a jungle-dweller. The public knows very little of these things anyway, for everyone is convinced that in our en-lightened society that kind of superstition has long since been eradicated, and it is part of the general convention to act as though one had never heard of such things, not to mention be-lieving in them.

481   But nothing is ever lost, not even the blood pact with the devil. Outwardly it is forgotten, but inwardly not at all. We act like the natives on the southern slopes of Mount Elgon, in East Africa, one of whom accompanied me part of the way into the bush. At a fork in the path we came upon a brand new "ghost trap," beautifully got up like a little hut, near the cave where

---

[15] Not to forget something means keeping it in consciousness. If the enemy disap-pears from my field of vision, then he may possibly be behind me—and even more dangerous.   [16] Radin, *The World of Primitive Man,* p. 3.   [17] Ibid., p. 5.

he lived with his family. I asked him if he had made it. He denied it with all the signs of extreme agitation, asserting that only children would make such a "ju-ju." Whereupon he gave the hut a kick, and the whole thing fell to pieces.

482   This is exactly the reaction we can observe in Europe today. Outwardly people are more or less civilized, but inwardly they are still primitives. Something in man is profoundly disinclined to give up his beginnings, and something else believes it has long since got beyond all that. This contradiction was once brought home to me in the most drastic manner when I was watching a "Strudel" (a sort of local witch-doctor) taking the spell off a stable. The stable was situated immediately beside the Gotthard railway line, and several international expresses sped past during the ceremony. Their occupants would hardly have suspected that a primitive ritual was being performed a few yards away.

483   The conflict between the two dimensions of consciousness is simply an expression of the polaristic structure of the psyche, which like any other energic system is dependent on the tension of opposites. That is also why there are no general psychological propositions which could not just as well be reversed; indeed, their reversibility proves their validity. We should never forget that in any psychological discussion we are not saying anything *about* the psyche, but that the psyche is always speaking about *itself*. It is no use thinking we can ever get beyond the psyche by means of the "mind," even though the mind asserts that it is not dependent on the psyche. How could it prove that? We can say, if we like, that one statement comes from the psyche, is psychic and nothing but psychic, and that another comes from the mind, is "spiritual" and therefore superior to the psychic one. Both are mere assertions based on the postulates of belief.

484   The fact is, that this old trichotomous hierarchy of psychic contents (hylic, psychic, and pneumatic) represents the polaristic structure of the psyche, which is the only immediate object of experience. The unity of our psychic nature lies in the middle, just as the living unity of the waterfall appears in the dynamic connection between above and below. Thus, the living effect of the myth is experienced when a higher consciousness, rejoicing in its freedom and independence, is confronted by the autonomy of a mythological figure and yet cannot flee from its

fascination, but must pay tribute to the overwhelming impression. The figure works, because secretly it participates in the observer's psyche and appears as its reflection, though it is not recognized as such. It is split off from his consciousness and consequently behaves like an autonomous personality. The trickster is a collective shadow figure, a summation of all the inferior traits of character in individuals. And since the individual shadow is never absent as a component of personality, the collective figure can construct itself out of it continually. Not always, of course, as a mythological figure, but, in consequence of the increasing repression and neglect of the original mythologems, as a corresponding projection on other social groups and nations.

485   If we take the trickster as a parallel of the individual shadow, then the question arises whether that trend towards meaning, which we saw in the trickster myth, can also be observed in the subjective and personal shadow. Since this shadow frequently appears in the phenomenology of dreams as a well-defined figure, we can answer this question positively: the shadow, although by definition a negative figure, sometimes has certain clearly discernible traits and associations which point to a quite different background. It is as though he were hiding meaningful contents under an unprepossessing exterior. Experience confirms this; and what is more important, the things that are hidden usually consist of increasingly numinous figures. The one standing closest behind the shadow is the anima,[18] who is endowed with considerable powers of fascination and possession. She often appears in rather too youthful form, and hides in her turn the powerful archetype of the wise old man (sage, magician, king, etc.). The series could be extended, but it would be pointless to do so, as psychologically one only understands what one has experienced oneself. The concepts of complex psychology are, in essence, not intellectual formula-

---

[18] By the metaphor "standing behind the shadow" I am attempting to illustrate the fact that, to the degree in which the shadow is recognized and integrated, the problem of the anima, i.e., of relationship, is constellated. It is understandable that the encounter with the shadow should have an enduring effect on the relations of the ego to the inside and outside world, since the integration of the shadow brings about an alteration of personality. Cf. *Aion*, Part II of this vol., pars. 13ff.

tions but names for certain areas of experience, and though they can be described they remain dead and irrepresentable to anyone who has not experienced them. Thus, I have noticed that people usually have not much difficulty in picturing to themselves what is meant by the shadow, even if they would have preferred instead a bit of Latin or Greek jargon that sounds more "scientific." But it costs them enormous difficulties to understand what the anima is. They accept her easily enough when she appears in novels or as a film star, but she is not understood at all when it comes to seeing the role she plays in their own lives, because she sums up everything that a man can never get the better of and never finishes coping with. Therefore it remains in a perpetual state of emotionality which must not be touched. The degree of unconsciousness one meets with in this connection is, to put it mildly, astounding. Hence it is practically impossible to get a man who is afraid of his own femininity to understand what is meant by the anima.

486   Actually, it is not surprising that this should be so, since even the most rudimentary insight into the shadow sometimes causes the greatest difficulties for the modern European. But since the shadow is the figure nearest his consciousness and the least explosive one, it is also the first component of personality to come up in an analysis of the unconscious. A minatory and ridiculous figure, he stands at the very beginning of the way of individuation, posing the deceptively easy riddle of the Sphinx, or grimly demanding answer to a "quaestio crocodilina." [19]

487   If, at the end of the trickster myth, the saviour is hinted at, this comforting premonition or hope means that some calamity or other has happened and been consciously understood. Only out of disaster can the longing for the saviour arise—in other words, the recognition and unavoidable integration of the shadow create such a harrowing situation that nobody but a saviour can undo the tangled web of fate. In the case of the individual, the problem constellated by the shadow is answered on the plane of the anima, that is, through relatedness. In the

[19] A crocodile stole a child from its mother. On being asked to give it back to her, the crocodile replied that he would grant her wish if she could give a true answer to his question: "Shall I give the child back?" If she answers "Yes," it is not true, and she won't get the child back. If she answers "No," it is again not true, so in either case the mother loses the child.

history of the collective as in the history of the individual, everything depends on the development of consciousness. This gradually brings liberation from imprisonment in ἀγνοία, 'unconsciousness,' [20] and is therefore a bringer of light as well as of healing.

488   As in its collective, mythological form, so also the individual shadow contains within it the seed of an enantiodromia, of a conversion into its opposite.

[20] Neumann, *The Origins and History of Consciousness*, passim.

BIBLIOGRAPHY

AELIAN. *De natura animalium*, etc. Edited by Rudolf Hercher. Paris, 1858.

AFANAS'EV, E. N. *Russian Fairy Tales*. Translated by Norbert Guterman. New York, [1946].

ALDROVANDUS, ULYSSES [Ulisse Aldrovandi]. *Dendrologiae libri duo*. Bologna, 1668; another edn., 1671.

AVALON, ARTHUR, pseud. (Sir John Woodroffe) (ed. and trans.) *The Serpent Power (Shat-chakra-nirupana and Paduka-panchaka)*. (Tantrik Texts.) London, 1919.

BELLOWS, HENRY ADAMS (trans.). *The Poetic Edda*. New York, 1923.

BERTHELOT, MARCELLIN. *Collection des anciens alchimistes grecs*. Paris, 1887-88. 3 vols.

BIN GORION, MICHA JOSEPH (pseud. of Micah Joseph Berdyczewski). *Der Born Judas*. Leipzig, 1916-23. 6 vols.

BOUSETT, WILHELM. *Hauptprobleme der Gnosis*. (Forschungen zur Religion und Literatur des Alten und Neuen Testaments, 10.) Göttingen, 1907.

BUDGE, E. A. WALLIS. *The Gods of the Egyptians*. London, 1904. 2 vols.

BURI, F. "Theologie und Philosophie," *Theologische Zeitschrift* (Basel), VIII (1952), 116-34.

CANTRIL, HADLEY. *The Invasion from Mars*. Princeton, 1940.

DU CANGE, CHARLES. *Glossarium ad scriptores mediae et infimae latinitatis*. Paris, 1733-36. 6 vols. New edn., Graz, 1954. 5 vols.

[ECKHART, MEISTER.] *Meister Eckhart*. By Franz Pfeiffer. Translated by C. de B. Evans. London, 1924-52. 2 vols.

[FIERZ-DAVID, LINDA.] *The Dream of Poliphilo.* Related and interpreted by Linda Fierz-David. Translated by Mary Hottinger. (Bollingen Series XXV.) New York, 1950.

FLAMEL, NICHOLAS. *Exposition of the Hieroglyphicall Figures . . .* Translated by Eirenaeus Orandus. London, 1624.

Folktales. (The following volumes are all from the series Die Märchen der Weltliteratur, edited by Friedrich von der Leyen and Paul Zaunert, Jena.)
Balkanmärchen aus Albanien, Bulgarien, Serbien und Kroatien. Edited by A. Laskien. 1915.
Chinesische Volksmärchen. Edited by R. Wilhelm. 1913.
Deutsche Märchen seit Grimm. Edited by Paul Zaunert. 1912.
Finnische und Estnische Volksmärchen. Edited by August von Löwis of Menar. 1922.
Indianermärchen aus Nordamerika. Edited by Walter Krickeberg. 1924.
Indianermärchen aus Südamerika. Edited by T. Koch-Grünberg. 1920.
Kaukasische Märchen. Edited by A. Dirr. 1919.
Märchen aus Iran. 1939.
Märchen aus Sibirien. 2nd edn., 1940.
Nordische Volksmärchen. Edited by K. Stroebe. 1915-22. 2 vols.
Russische Volksmärchen. Edited by August von Löwis of Menar. 1914.
Spanische und Portugiesische Märchen. Edited by Harri Meier. 1940.
See also AFANAS'EV; GRIMM.

GARBE, RICHARD. *Die Samkhya Philosophie.* Leipzig, 1894.

GOETHE, JOHANN WOLFGANG VON. "Die neue Melusine." See *Wilhelm Meisters Wanderjahre,* in *Werke,* q.v., VIII, pp. 380ff.

———. *Faust, Part One.* Translated by Philip Wayne. (Penguin Classics.) Harmondsworth, 1949.

———. *Werke.* (Gedenkausgabe.) Edited by Ernst Beutler. Zurich, 1948-54. 24 vols. (Vols. I–II: *Sämtliche Gedichte.*)

GOETZ, BRUNO. *Das Reich ohne Raum.* Potsdam, 1919. 2nd enl. edn., Constance, 1925.

GRIMM, THE BROTHERS. *Fairy Tales*. Translated by Margaret Hunt. Revised by James Stern. New York, 1944.

HOLLANDUS, JOANNES ISAACS. *Opera mineralia*. Middelburg, 1600.

Homeric Hymns. See: *Hesiod, the Homeric Hymns, and Homerica*. With an English translation by Hugh G. Evelyn-White. (Loeb Classical Library.) London and New York, 1914.

HORNEFFER, ERNST. *Nietzsches Lehre von der ewigen Wiederkunft*. Leipzig, 1900.

Hovamol. See BELLOWS.

HUME, ROBERT ERNEST (trans.). *The Thirteen Principal Upanishads*. Oxford, 1921. (Shvetashvatara Upanishad, pp. 394-411.)

I Ching, or Book of Changes. The German translation by Richard Wilhelm, rendered into English by Cary F. Baynes. New York (Bollingen Series XIX) and London, 1950; 3rd edn., Princeton and London, 1967.

IRENAEUS, SAINT. *Adversus* [or *Contra*] *haereses libri quinque*. See MIGNE, *P.G.*, vol. 7, cols. 433-1224. For translation, see: *The Writings of Irenaeus*. Translated by Alexander Roberts and W. H. Rambaut. (Ante-Nicene Christian Library, 5, 9.) Edinburgh, 1868. 2 vols.

IZQUIERDO, SEBASTIAN. *Pratica di alcuni Esercitij Spirituali di S. Ignatio*. Rome, 1686.

JACOBSOHN, HELMUTH. "Die dogmatische Stellung des Königs in der Theologie der alten Aegypter," *Aegyptologische Forschungen* (Glückstadt), no. 8 (1939).

JANET, PIERRE. *Les Névroses*. Paris, 1909.

JUNG, CARL GUSTAV. *Aion: Researches into the Phenomenology of the Self. Collected Works,** Vol. 9, Part II. Princeton and London, 2nd edn., 1968.

———. *Alchemical Studies. Collected Works*, Vol. 13. Princeton and London, 1968.

* For details of the *Collected Works of C. G. Jung*, see end of this volume.

———. *Civilization in Transition. Collected Works*, Vol. 10. Princeton and London, 2nd edn., 1970.

———. "Instinct and the Unconscious." In: *The Structure and Dynamics of the Psyche*, q.v.

———. *Mysterium Coniunctionis. Collected Works*, Vol. 14. Princeton and London, 2nd edn., 1970.

———. "On the Nature of the Psyche." In: *The Structure and Dynamics of the Psyche*, q.v.

———. "On the Psychology and Pathology of So-called Occult Phenomena." In: *Psychiatric Studies*, q.v.

———. "Paracelsus as a Spiritual Phenomenon." In: *Alchemical Studies*, q.v.

———. *The Practice of Psychotherapy. Collected Works*, Vol. 16. Princeton and London, 2nd edn., 1966.

———. *Psychiatric Studies. Collected Works*, Vol. 1. Princeton and London, 2nd edn., 1970.

———. "A Psychological Approach to the Dogma of the Trinity." In: *Psychology and Religion: West and East*, q.v.

———. *Psychological Types. Collected Works*, Vol. 6. Princeton and London, 1971.

———. *Psychology and Alchemy. Collected Works*, Vol. 12. Princeton and London, 2nd edn., 1968.

———. "The Psychology of Eastern Meditation." In: *Psychology and Religion: West and East*, q.v.

———. "Psychology and Religion" (The Terry Lectures). In: *Psychology and Religion: West and East*, q.v.

———. *Psychology and Religion: West and East. Collected Works*, Vol. 11. Princeton and London, 2nd edn., 1969.

———. "The Psychology of the Transference." In: *The Practice of Psychotherapy*, q.v. See also Princeton/Bollingen Paperback no. 158 (1969).

———. "The Spirit Mercurius." In: *Alchemical Studies*, q.v.

———. *The Structure and Dynamics of the Psyche. Collected Works,* Vol. 8. Princeton and London, 2nd edn., 1969.

———. *Symbols of Transformation. Collected Works,* Vol. 5. Princeton and London, 2nd edn., 1967.

———. "Synchronicity: An Acausal Connecting Phenomenon." In: *The Structure and Dynamics of the Psyche,* q.v.

———. "Transformation Symbolism in the Mass." In: *Psychology and Religion: West and East,* q.v.

———. *Two Essays on Analytical Psychology. Collected Works,* Vol. 7. Princeton and London, 2nd edn., 1966.

———. "The Visions of Zosimos." In: *Alchemical Studies,* q.v.

———. "Wotan." In: *Civilization in Transition,* q.v.

——— and KERÉNYI, C. *Essays on a Science of Mythology.* (Bollingen Series XXII.) New York, 1949. (Also pub. as *Introduction to a Science of Mythology,* London, 1950.) See also Princeton/Bollingen Paperback no. 180 (1969).

JUNG, EMMA. "On the Nature of the Animus." Translated by Cary F. Baynes, in: *Animus and Anima.* (The Analytical Psychology Club of New York.) New York, 1957.

KEYSERLING, HERMANN COUNT VON. *South-American Meditations.* Translated by Therese Duerr. New York and London, 1932. (Original: *Südamerikanische Meditationen.* Stuttgart, 1932.)

KLAGES, LUDWIG. *Der Geist als Widersacher der Seele.* Leipzig, 1929-32. 3 vols.

KÖHLER, REINHOLD. *Kleinere Schriften zur Märchenforschung.* Weimar, 1898.

Koran, The. Translated by N. J. Dawood. (Penguin Classics.) Harmondsworth, 1956.

LE BON, GUSTAVE. *The Crowd.* 19th impr., London, 1947. (English version first published 1896.)

LÉVY-BRUHL, LUCIEN. *La Mythologie primitive.* Paris, 1935.

McGLASHAN, ALAN. "Daily Paper Pantheon," *The Lancet* (London), vol. 264(i) (1953), 238-39.

MIGNE, JACQUES PAUL (ed.). *Patrologiae cursus completus.* [*P.L.*] Latin series. Paris, 1844-64. 221 vols. [*P.G.*] Greek series, Paris, 1857–66. 166 vols. (These works are referred to in the text as "Migne, *P.L.*," and "Migne, *P.G.*," respectively.)

MYLIUS, JOHANN DANIEL. *Philosophia reformata.* Frankfurt a. M., 1622.

NEUMANN, ERICH. *The Origins and History of Consciousness.* New York (Bollingen Series XLII) and London, 1954. See also Princeton/Bollingen Paperback no. 204 (1970).

NIETZSCHE, FRIEDRICH. *Thus Spake Zarathustra.* Translated by Thomas Common, revised by Oscar Levy and John L. Beevers. London, 1932.

———. *Gedichte und Sprüche.* Leipzig, 1898.

NINCK, MARTIN. *Wodan und germanischer Schicksalsglaube.* Jena, 1935.

PRUDENTIUS. *Contra Symmachum.* In: [*Works.*] With an English translation by H. J. Thomson. (Loeb Classical Library.) London and Cambridge, Mass., 1949–53. (Vol. I, p. 344–Vol. II, p. 97.)

RADIN, PAUL. *The World of Primitive Man.* New York, 1953.

RAHNER, HUGO. "Earth Spirit and Divine Spirit in Patristic Theology." In: *Spirit and Nature.* (Papers from the Eranos Yearbooks, 1.) Translated by Ralph Manheim. New York (Bollingen Series XXX), 1954; London, 1955.

———. "Die seelenheilende Blume," *Eranos Jahrbuch* (Zurich), XII (C. G. Jung Festgabe, 1945), 117–239.

REITZENSTEIN, RICHARD. *Poimandres.* Leipzig, 1904.

RHINE, J. B. *New Frontiers of the Mind.* London, 1937.

RICHARD OF ST. VICTOR. *Benjamin minor.* In MIGNE, *P.L.*, vol. 196, cols. 1–64.

RIPLEY, SIR GEORGE. "Cantilena." In: *Opera omnia chemica.* Kassel, 1649.

Rosarium philosophorum. Secunda pars alchimiae de lapide philosophico. Frankfurt a. M., 1550.

RULAND, MARTIN. *A Lexicon of Alchemy.* [London, 1893.] (Original: *Lexicon alchemiae.* Frankfurt a. M., 1612.)

Samyutta-Nikaya. See: *The Book of the Kindred Sayings (Sangyutta-Nikaya).* Part II: *The Nidana Book (Nidana-Vagga).* Translated by Mrs. C. A. F. Rhys Davids. London, [1922]. Also: *Dialogues of the Buddha.* Part II. Translated by T. W. and C. A. F. Rhys Davids. (Sacred Books of the Buddhists. 3.) London, 1951.

[SAND, GEORGE] *Intimate Journal of George Sand.* Translated and edited by Marie Jenney Howe. New York, 1929.

SCHOPENHAUER, ARTHUR. *Aphorismen zur Lebensweisheit.* Translated in: *Essays from the Parerga and Paralipomena.* Translated by T. Bailey Saunders. London, 1951. ("The Wisdom of Life," in section "The Art of Controversy," pp. 56–71.) (Original in: *Sämmtliche Werke.* Edited by Julius Frauenstädt. Vol. V: *Parerga und Paralipomena,* 1. Leipzig, 1877.)

SPENCER, SIR WALTER R., and GILLEN, FRANCIS JAMES. *The Northern Tribes of Central Australia.* London, 1904.

TERTULLIAN. *Apologeticus adversus gentes.* See MIGNE, *P.L.*, vol. 1, cols. 257–536.

TONQUÉDEC, JOSEPH DE. *Les Maladies nerveuses ou mentales et les manifestations diaboliques.* Paris, 1938.

USENER, HERMANN. *Das Weihnachtsfest.* 2nd edn., Bonn, 1911.

VOLLERS, K. "Chidher," *Archiv für Religionswissenschaft* (Leipzig), XII (1909), 234–384.

WARNECKE, JOHANNES. *Die Religion der Batak.* Leipzig, 1909.

WECKERLING, ADOLF (trans.). *Ananda-raya-makhi. Das Glück des*

Lebens. (Arbeiten der deutsch-nordischen Gesellschaft für Geschichte der Medizin, der Zahnheilkunde und der Nervenwissenschaften, 13.) Greifswald, 1937.

WELLS, HERBERT GEORGE. *The War of the Worlds.* London, 1898.

WILLIAMS, MENTOR L. (ed.). *Schoolcraft's Indian Legends.* East Lansing, Michigan, 1956.

WYLIE, PHILIP. *Generation of Vipers.* New York, 1942.

INDEX

A

abaissement du niveau mental, 53, 54, 73
ablution, 63
Acts of the Apostles, 143
Adam, Second, 68*n*, 75
Aelian, 114*n*
Afanas'ev, E. N., 120*n*
Africa, East, 29; *see also* Kenya
albedo, 74*n*
alchemists/alchemy, 67, 75*n*; Chinese, and fish, 74, and prolongation of life, 70; and spirit, 86, 93; triad in, 112; and union of opposites, 43
alcheringamijina, 59, 60*n*
alcohol, 87
Aldrovandus, Ulysses, 58*n*
Alexander the Great, 78, 79
Amnesias, 54
anaesthetic areas, 54
ancestors, identification with, 60
ancestral: roles, 58; souls, 59
ancestress, 15
Ancient of Days, 104
angel(s): fallen, 92; first, 77
angelos, 77
anima, 57, 117*f*, 120, 122*ff*, 150*f*; an archetype, 16, 28; derivation, 87; as Mercurius, 90*n*; old man as, 107; possession caused by, 58; as soul, 89
anima mundi, 114
animal(s), archetype as, 94; in fairytales, 99, 108*f*; helpful, 109, 120; poltergeist as, 136; psyche of, 59; talking, 93
animosity, 28

animus, 125; derivation, 87; old man as, 107; "positive," 93; possession by, 58; represents spirit, 122
Anthroparion, 101
Antichrist, 75
ape of God, 135
Apollo, 114*n*
apparition, 92*n*
apple(s), 101, 106
Apuleius, 41, 62
aqua permanens, 74
arbor philosophica, 129*n*
archetype(s), dynamism of, 36; mother as carrier of, 36; origin of, 35; positive and negative sides, 104; relatively autonomous, 100; *see also* anima; animus; father; mother; self; shadow; wise old man
Aristotle, 9; Aristotelian reasoning, 10
Ars chemica, 67*n*
Artis auriferae, 68*n*, 74*n*, 75*n*
ascension, of Christ, 48
asses: feast of, 138
Assumption, *see* Mary, the Virgin
Astrampsychos, 67*n*
Aswan, 68
Athi plains, 29
athla, 119
Atlantis, 143
atman/Atman, 76, 102; atomic fission, 131; atomic world, 102
attitude, 116; conscious, onesidedness of, 73
Augustine, St., 9
"Aurea hora," 68*n*
Australian aborigines, 60*n*; and ancestors, 59

THE COLLECTED WORKS OF

C. G. JUNG

THE PUBLICATION of the first complete edition, in English, of the works of C. G. Jung was undertaken by Routledge and Kegan Paul, Ltd., in England and by Bollingen Foundation in the United States. The American edition is number XX in Bollingen Series, which since 1967 has been published by Princeton University Press. The edition contains revised versions of works previously published, such as *Psychology of the Unconscious*, which is now entitled *Symbols of Transformation*; works originally written in English, such as *Psychology and Religion*; works not previously translated, such as *Aion*; and, in general, new translations of virtually all of Professor Jung's writings. Prior to his death, in 1961, the author supervised the textual revision, which in some cases is extensive. Sir Herbert Read (d. 1968), Dr. Michael Fordham, and Dr. Gerhard Adler (d. 1988) compose the Editorial Committee; the translator is R. F. C. Hull (except for Volume 2) and William McGuire is executive editor.

The price of the volumes varies according to size; they are sold separately, and may also be obtained on standing order. Several of the volumes are extensively illustrated. Each volume contains an index and, in most cases, a bibliography; the final volumes contain a complete bibliography of Professor Jung's writings and a general index to the entire edition.

In the following list, dates of original publication are given in parentheses (of original composition, in brackets). Multiple dates indicate revisions.

* Published 1960.   † Published 1961.
‡ Published 1956; 2nd edn., 1967. (65 plates, 43 text figures.)

Psychological Factors Determining Human Behavior (1937)
Instinct and the Unconscious (1919)
The Structure of the Psyche (1927/1931)
On the Nature of the Psyche (1947/1954)
General Aspects of Dream Psychology (1916/1948)
On the Nature of Dreams (1945/1948)
The Psychological Foundations of Belief in Spirits (1920/1948)
Spirit and Life (1926)
Basic Postulates of Analytical Psychology (1931)
Analytical Psychology and *Weltanschauung* (1928/1931)
The Real and the Surreal (1933)
The Stages of Life (1930–1931)
The Soul and Death (1934)
Synchronicity: An Acausal Connecting Principle (1952)
Appendix: On Synchronicity (1951)

*9. PART I. THE ARCHETYPES AND THE
   COLLECTIVE UNCONSCIOUS
Archetypes of the Collective Unconscious (1934/1954)
The Concept of the Collective Unconscious (1936)
Concerning the Archetypes, with Special Reference to the Anima
   Concept (1936/1954)
Psychological Aspects of the Mother Archetype (1938/1954)
Concerning Rebirth (1940/1950)
The Psychology of the Child Archetype (1940)
The Psychological Aspects of the Kore (1941)
The Phenomenology of the Spirit in Fairytales (1945/1948)
On the Psychology of the Trickster-Figure (1954)
Conscious, Unconscious, and Individuation (1939)
A Study in the Process of Individuation (1934/1950)
Concerning Mandala Symbolism (1950)
Appendix: Mandalas (1955)

*9. PART II. AION (1951)
   RESEARCHES INTO THE PHENOMENOLOGY OF THE SELF
The Ego
The Shadow
The Syzygy: Anima and Animus
The Self
Christ, a Symbol of the Self
The Sign of the Fishes   (*continued*)

* Published 1959; 2nd edn., 1968. (Part I: 79 plates, with 29 in colour.)

* Published 1964; 2nd edn., 1970. (8 plates.)
† Published 1958; 2nd edn., 1969.

A Psychological Approach to the Dogma of the Trinity (1942/1948)
Transformation Symbolism in the Mass (1942/1954)
Forewords to White's "God and the Unconscious" and Werblowsky's "Lucifer and Prometheus" (1952)
Brother Klaus (1933)
Psychotherapists or the Clergy (1932)
Psychoanalysis and the Cure of Souls (1928)
Answer to Job (1952)

EASTERN RELIGION

Psychological Commentaries on "The Tibetan Book of the Great Liberation" (1939/1954) and "The Tibetan Book of the Dead" (1935/1953)
Yoga and the West (1936)
Foreword to Suzuki's "Introduction to Zen Buddhism" (1939)
The Psychology of Eastern Meditation (1943)
The Holy Men of India: Introduction to Zimmer's "Der Weg zum Selbst" (1944)
Foreword to the "I Ching" (1950)

*12. PSYCHOLOGY AND ALCHEMY (1944)
Prefatory note to the English Edition ([1951?] added 1967)
Introduction to the Religious and Psychological Problems of Alchemy
Individual Dream Symbolism in Relation to Alchemy (1936)
Religious Ideas in Alchemy (1937)
Epilogue

†13. ALCHEMICAL STUDIES
Commentary on "The Secret of the Golden Flower" (1929)
The Visions of Zosimos (1938/1954)
Paracelsus as a Spiritual Phenomenon (1942)
The Spirit Mercurius (1943/1948)
The Philosophical Tree (1945/1954)

‡14. MYSTERIUM CONIUNCTIONIS (1955-56)
AN INQUIRY INTO THE SEPARATION AND
SYNTHESIS OF PSYCHIC OPPOSITES IN ALCHEMY
The Components of the Coniunctio
The Paradoxa
The Personification of the Opposites
Rex and Regina   (continued)

* Published 1953; 2nd edn., completely revised, 1968. (270 illustrations.)
† Published 1968. (50 plates, 4 text figures.)
‡ Published 1963; 2nd edn., 1970. (10 plates.)

* Published 1966.
† Published 1954; 2nd edn., revised and augmented, 1966. (13 illustrations.)
‡ Published 1954.